MARILYN BELL

MARILYN BELL

The Heart-Stopping Tale of
Marilyn's Record-Breaking Swim

SPORT/HUMAN INTEREST

by Patrick Tivy

PUBLISHED BY ALTITUDE PUBLISHING CANADA LTD.
1500 Railway Avenue, Canmore, Alberta T1W 1P6
www.altitudepublishing.com
1-800-957-6888

Publisher	Stephen Hutchings
Associate Publisher	Kara Turner
Editor	Jay Winans
Digital Photo Colouring	Scott Manktelow

We acknowledge the financial support of the Government
of Canada through the Book Publishing Industry Development
Program (BPIDP) for our publishing activities.

Altitude GreenTree Program
Altitude Publishing will plant twice as many trees as were used
in the manufacturing of this product.

National Library of Canada Cataloguing in Publication Data

Tivy, Patrick, 1945-
Marilyn Bell / Patrick Tivy.

(Amazing stories)
Includes bibliographical references.
ISBN 1-55153-964-0

1. Bell, Marilyn, 1937- 2. Swimmers--Canada--Biography.
I. Title. II. Series: Amazing stories (Canmore, Alta.)

GV838.B4T57 2003   797.2'1'092   C2003-905472-1

An application for the trademark for Amazing Stories™
has been made and the registered trademark is pending.

Printed and bound in Canada by Friesens
2 4 6 8 9 7 5 3

Cover: Marilyn Bell after her historic swim

To all strong and inspiring women, especially my dear mother Mary, my darling daughters Jessica and Robin, my beloved wife Valerie and, of course, to Marilyn Bell.

Contents

Prologue

The girl in the water was all alone. Hundreds of shouting onlookers were circling about in boats. Thousands were cheering on the shore. Millions more across the country were listening to radio broadcasts and reading newspaper stories about Marilyn Bell, the 16-year-old girl who was moments away from becoming the first person ever to swim across Lake Ontario.

Yet Marilyn saw nothing and heard nothing. She didn't know that the largest crowd ever assembled in Toronto was cheering for her. Nor could she know that frantic teams of newspaper reporters were anxiously waiting for her, some of them even plotting to kidnap her to get her story. Marilyn had been swimming for almost 21 hours and was exhausted. Her stomach ached and her legs felt like lead. She felt she had been swimming forever. She would have cried, but no more tears would come. She was too tired to weep any more.

There were only a few voices Marilyn could hear, the voices of friends on a nearby boat. The loudest was Gus

Ryder, the man she called "my wonderful trainer." All along, Gus had called out, urging her forward, demanding that she finish. "Come on," Gus yelled, "keep going!"

Suddenly the breakwater was just one stroke away. The moment Marilyn touched it her swim would be over and her agony would end. It was then she finally noticed the people cheering around her. She saw their faces in a flash of light, and a tremendous shiver shook her entire body. Somehow she found a new surge of strength. With one final effort Marilyn extended her left hand all the way, reaching out to touch the breakwater, closer, closer, closer....

Chapter 1

I Did It for Canada

Marilyn Bell dived into darkness — and into Canadian history — at 11:07 p.m. on Wednesday, September 8, 1954. It was a clean dive from a log retaining wall by the dock at the U.S. Coast Guard Station at Youngstown, New York. As she splashed into Lake Ontario she felt the warmth of the water embrace her. She began swimming fast; it was better to be swimming than sitting around waiting in the rain. She was tired of waiting. It was time to get going. But still it was a bit strange and frightening to be swimming at night. Marilyn had never done it before, but she didn't let that stop her. Now that she was 16, she had learned to make it a habit to dive right in and do things.

Marilyn wasn't alone in the darkness. There was a boat, the *Mipepa*, waiting for her not far from the shore, she was sure of that. Operating the *Mipepa* was Jack Russell, a cheerful professional boatman who steered the boat and was in charge of the motor. Just a few minutes before Marilyn dove in, Jack had given Marilyn a good luck charm, a genuine four-leaf clover. She'd folded up the sweet little gift in a protective piece of waxed paper and set it right on top of her head, then she'd pulled on her white rubber swimming cap, and tugged it tight. All girls wore swimming caps then, especially if they were serious about swimming.

Gus Ryder was in the *Mipepa*, too. Gus was the reason Marilyn was in the lake. He was one of the most inspiring individuals in Toronto sports history. For more than 20 years he'd been running the Lakeshore Swimming Club and had taught thousands of youngsters to swim. Gus was a determined teacher. In the early days of the club, if he couldn't find a public swimming pool that could handle his classes, he'd teach the swimmers right there on the banks of the Credit River. Also in the boat was a newspaper reporter from the *Toronto Star*, George Bryant, and a boy, Peter Willinsky, who was the son of Dr. Bernard Willinsky, the man who owned the *Mipepa* and also the *Mona IV*, the yacht that Marilyn's parents were following in. Young Peter was already an experienced boater and had helped Jack load all the supplies into the *Mipepa*.

Like Jack, Gus also had a brief conversation with Marilyn before the race began, but it was much more than a last-minute pep talk. Gus knew they were both about to confront one of the greatest challenges of their lives, and they'd need all the help they could get. Gus would soon leave to get in the *Mipepa*, but before he went he said there was something very special that Marilyn should do just before she started her swim. She should say a little prayer. "Kneel," said Gus, "and ask the Greatest Coach and Instructor for divine guidance and strength to make this voyage, and in our boat waiting for you we will do the same." After Gus left, Marilyn waited for the right moment for her private prayer. There was a crowd of people milling around the dock at the Coast Guard Station, but hardly anyone noticed her bend down on one knee and bow her head. Then she got up again, gave her mother and father each one last kiss, and set off in the dark on her fabulous journey across almost 52 kilometres of open water.

It surprised Marilyn how many people there were who turned out to see her swim across Lake Ontario. After all, she'd been swimming for years at the

Lakeshore Swimming Club and had been winning medals, with scarcely a flicker of interest from the public at all. And in fact, most of the reporters and photographers at the Coast Guard Station really weren't there to see Marilyn at all. They were there to see the great Florence Chadwick.

As far as most of the reporters and photographers were concerned, Marilyn Bell was just a 16-year-old girl who'd won a race or two. But Florence Chadwick was famous, an international swimming superstar. Everyone knew Florence Chadwick was the very best woman long-distance swimmer in the world. She was the first woman swimmer to cross the English Channel both ways — from France to England in 1950, then from England to France in 1951 — setting records each way. Now a veteran athlete of 34, Florence Chadwick didn't need to set any more world records. She had come to Lake Ontario because of an enticing and lucrative offer from the CNE.

The CNE was the biggest fair in all of Canada, and certainly the biggest summer party in Toronto. Hardly anyone ever bothered to call the CNE by its full name, the Canadian National Exhibition; it was always just "the CNE" or, shorter still, "the Ex." For many years, the CNE had presented swimming races along the shores of Lake Ontario, including full-scale marathon races. This year, however, the CNE directors decided to do something different to entertain fairgoers. They offered Florence Chadwick a special prize of $10,000 if she would swim from the New York side of Lake Ontario all the way across to the CNE grounds. For Florence Chadwick it looked like easy money. Under the arrangement, she picked up $2500 to start with and would pick up the rest at the finish line.

But not everyone thought it was such a good idea. Some swimmers — and Marilyn Bell was one of them — thought it was a downright shame that there wasn't going to be a marathon race at the Ex; Marilyn had been looking forward to it. Others thought it wasn't quite right to be giving all that money to someone who wasn't even a Canadian. After all, $10,000 was enough to buy a house in 1954. Florence Chadwick was from San Diego, California, and had performed in Hollywood movies.

The CNE directors weren't happy with the criticism, so they welcomed plans for a relay race for other swimmers. The relay race would take place at the same time Florence Chadwick was making her solo effort across the lake. Marilyn wanted to be on one of the relay teams, but instead was offered a spot as a substitute. She would only take part if one of the other members needed to be replaced. Then she got the idea of going it alone, all the way. She wanted to turn Florence

Chadwick's solo stunt into a real race.

"I don't think I was sure I could make it," Marilyn said later, "but I wasn't so sure Florence Chadwick could make it either."

Marilyn was young, but she had been in enough races to know that things don't always go the way they're planned. "The challenge for me was to go one stroke further than the American. As corny as it sounds," she said, "I did it for Canada."

She knew she couldn't do it without the help of one person in particular. She went straight to him. "I'd love to swim against Florence Chadwick across the lake, Gus," she told him. Gus Ryder was not a man to waste words. He was silent as he looked directly into Marilyn's eyes. "All right, Marilyn," he said. "If your parents agree, I'm all for it. It's up to you." Marilyn knew that meant she could do it — because she knew if Gus Ryder said it was okay, Mom and Dad would too.

Marilyn wasn't Florence Chadwick's only challenger. Also ready to compete was Winnie Roach Leuszler, 28, one of the best swimmers in Ontario. Just three years earlier, Winnie too had swum the English Channel. The fact that the two new swimmers were both Canadians who wanted to compete against an American star caught the public's attention. Sympathy for them spread far and wide, especially when the CNE announced that there would be no additional money for either Winnie or Marilyn. Local business operators came forward with welcome donations to help pay for expenses. A man who had a jewelry store said he would present Marilyn with $1000 if she could make it. Then a hardware store owner stepped up and donated $100. "I think it's a real shame a Canadian girl is offered nothing," said the hardware store owner, "when Miss Chadwick stands to win ten thousand for the swim."

It was a substantial sum — certainly $100 was much more than most working people earned in a week, but Gus knew they'd need much more support. Gus was a customs broker when he wasn't teaching someone to swim. As a successful businessman, he knew which doors to knock on. One of the first persons he went to was John Bassett, the publisher of *The Telegram*, one of Toronto's most popular newspapers. "The *Tely*," as it was often called, presented itself as the champion of the underdog and always had room for a great "human interest" story. Gus wanted to work out a straightforward business deal with the *Tely* — in exchange for a $5000 sponsorship for expenses, the newspaper would have exclusive rights to Marilyn's story. It was a fateful meeting, one that would lead to a bizarre sequence of hare-brained events that began as Marilyn was struggling to complete her race across Lake Ontario. The wild stunts received very little publicity at the time, but they became the stuff of legend in newspaper offices across the land.

John Bassett knew all about Gus and his accomplishments with the boys and girls at the Lakeshore Swimming Club. And as a veteran newspaper publisher, he also was very aware of the appeal of Marilyn's challenge. But Bassett didn't share Gus Ryder's confidence in Marilyn. She was 16, just a kid. She couldn't compete with the likes of Florence Chadwick, a grown woman and a renowned champion. And he was concerned about what would happen to his newspaper's reputation if anything went wrong.

"Gus," he said, "a 16-year-old girl, swimming Lake Ontario? The *Tely* can't be part of that. It's not the money … but it's cruelty to children.

"In any event, you'll have to pull her out halfway across. No, Gus, I can't do it."

Gus was disappointed, but the *Tely* wasn't the only newspaper in town. Gus went instead to the *Toronto Star*, where his proposal was welcomed. That's why George Bryant was also in the boat that night with Gus, Jack, and young Peter. George was a "two-way man" with the *Star*, a reporter who was also a photographer. The involvement of the *Star* created much more media interest. Radio stations would report the swim, too.

Television reporters would have liked to follow the swim as well, but TV equipment in those days was very heavy and complicated to operate — so there could be no television broadcasts from the lakeshore. However, there were plenty of newsreel photographers who were filming short items that would be shown at movie theatres around the world.

The small brigade of reporters and photographers congregated at Youngstown, all of them anxious for Florence Chadwick, Winnie Roach Leuszler, and Marilyn to begin their swim. The three women — well, two women and one schoolgirl — had gathered there with their friends and supporters, waiting for the start of a race that wasn't supposed to be a race at all. Because of her contract with the CNE, Florence Chadwick had a tremendous advantage over her competitors. The contract gave her the exclusive right to decide when she would start her swim across the lake. Winnie and Marilyn could only wait for Florence to decide — and wait they did, day after day, hour after frustrating hour.

Florence Chadwick originally said she planned to start on Monday night, but the weather was stormy and wet, so she called it off. Tuesday was just as bad. Wednesday started out rough, but hour by hour the skies cleared. It looked like the lake might be all right after all. Trouble was, no one knew what Florence

Chadwick thought of it — they could only guess and wonder. The guessing stopped at 9:30 p.m., Wednesday night. Florence Chadwick announced to the world that the time had come. She would start her swim at 11 p.m. — that gave Winnie and Marilyn just 90 minutes to get ready.

Winnie was delayed for some reason, but Marilyn was well prepared. She was in her Lakeshore swimsuit, sitting patiently by the log retaining wall when Florence Chadwick emerged from a Coast Guard building. An honour guard of U.S. soldiers in full uniform escorted the famous swimming actress to the water's edge. Florence Chadwick jumped in the water at precisely 11:06 and immediately started swimming for the Ontario side of the lake. A Coast Guard spotlight was shining on her, showing the speed she had with her strong, graceful stroke. She was such a beautiful sight in the water that the crowd on the dock cheered. Marilyn gave her opponent a 60-second head start, then joined the race.

There were some on the dock who didn't see Marilyn dive into the lake, but they heard the splash. Now there were two beautiful swimmers in the lake. Marilyn was trying hard to swim faster, swimming like a sprinter, so she could get ahead of Florence Chadwick. Marilyn wanted to get in front and then stay there. She wasn't worried as much about Winnie, because Winnie still hadn't arrived at the Coast Guard Station.

The crowd on the dock watched the two swimmers in the spotlight grow smaller and smaller as they sped away, stroke by stroke, from the New York side of the lake. After a while, there was nothing to see but the waves, and many in the crowd went away.

After days of inaction Marilyn was in great shape. She hadn't rested as much as she should have on Wednesday, but she was filled with excitement. It was so different swimming in the dark — somehow it was quieter. Swimming now was good. She could feel the water washing by her body, feel her hands and legs pushing it back. Each stroke, each kick, put her closer to other side of the lake.

There was only one thing wrong — she didn't want her eye goggles on. She didn't need them. Without missing a stroke, she pulled them from her face and threw them as far as she could. All Marilyn needed was to find Gus. She was sure she'd see him soon.

Chapter 2
That's the Way to Swim, Kid!

Surrounded by darkness, Marilyn kept up the astonishing burst of speed. It was a bit confusing swimming at night; she couldn't be sure she was going in the right direction. Toronto was almost 52 kilometres away, and she knew she'd never make it without Gus. But she didn't have to worry long. Suddenly she heard a calm, familiar voice calling out to her. It was Gus! "This way, Marilyn," Gus said. "This way!" Then she saw the light bobbing on the back of the boat and swam quickly toward it. With Gus coaching her from the *Mipepa*, Marilyn was certain she could make it all the way.

The 16-year-old schoolgirl and the 55-year-old

coach had formed a remarkable partnership, one that brought out the best in both of them. Right at the very start of her race against Florence Chadwick and Winnie Roach Leuszler, it was easy to see how important that teamwork was to Marilyn. When Florence had announced just a few hours earlier that she had decided to begin her swim to the CNE, Marilyn and Gus were both completely prepared. The young swimmer and her experienced trainer had worked out Marilyn's starting sprint strategy, and both knew how important it was for Marilyn to find the boat as soon as she could.

The other challenger in the race, Winnie Roach Leuszler, wasn't as well organized. Winnie and her trainers had the same 90-minute warning that Florence Chadwick was about to start her swim, but Winnie wasn't able to get to the Coast Guard dock in time to start with Florence and Marilyn. Even worse, when Winnie finally did arrive at the dock, things went very badly for her. She dived into the lake 17 minutes after Marilyn's start, strong and confident and fully expecting to catch up with the other swimmers. But Winnie got thoroughly lost in the darkness. The black night and the tossing waves made it impossible for her to figure out which way to go. Winnie couldn't see the guide boat that was supposed to be waiting for her — and the crew in the boat couldn't see her. Winnie swam first in one direction, then had to stop and swim in another, all in the vain hope of finding her guide boat. But every direction she chose was the wrong direction. Eventually, frustrated and exasperated, she realized the only thing she could do was go back. And so she turned and swam back to the bright lights on the Coast Guard dock, and there she finally found her guide boat.

Winnie wasted almost an hour thrashing around in the darkness before she and her guide boat were able to set off on the proper course across Lake Ontario. For Winnie, it was truly a disastrous start to the race. And, for her, it would get much worse.

For Marilyn and Gus, though, things were going, well, swimmingly. Marilyn stayed focused on her pace. She was swimming at a steady 64 strokes per minute. Gus and the others in the boat kept cheering her on. Soon, Marilyn was sure, she would pull ahead of Florence Chadwick. This was a race she knew she could win — thanks to her strength, thanks to her determination, and thanks to her trainer, Gus.

Marilyn and Gus had a lot in common, despite the vast difference in their ages. They both had discovered something about swimming that they couldn't find anywhere else in their lives. Marilyn and Gus both felt a bond to water that most people would never understand.

That's the Way to Swim, Kid!

Marilyn and Gus were Torontonians, even though Marilyn had spent many years of her short life in other cities. Marilyn Grace Bell was born on October 19, 1937, in Toronto. Her parents were Sydney and Grace Bell. "Syd," as her father was generally called, was an ambitious and lucky man. The Great Depression had put thousands of men out of work across Canada, but Syd had a good job as an accounting clerk with Dominion Stores, a prosperous company that was growing rapidly. Not long after Marilyn's second birthday, Syd got an important promotion that meant a move to the distant city of North Bay in northern Ontario. The young family barely got to know their new home; after just two years, Syd was transferred to Halifax. It was there in 1944 that another girl joined the family as Marilyn got a sister, Karen.

Marilyn liked Halifax and had fun at school, taking part in several school plays. But the Bell family was not through moving yet. Halifax had been a bustling place during the Second World War, but after peace came in 1945, it changed as all the soldiers and sailors left the port so they could return to their homes elsewhere in the country. And within a few short months, the Bells were ready to join the exodus out of Halifax. They were going to return to Ontario. The family was coming home to Toronto.

Marilyn Bell

Marilyn and her family arrived back in Toronto in January, 1946, and found the city in the midst of a housing shortage. The war had brought thousands of people to the city, either to military bases or to the city's factories or offices, but there weren't enough houses for them all. Toronto was simply growing too fast. Marilyn's parents searched high and low but couldn't find a place to live right away. Eventually, of course, they settled in a home in the western suburb of New Toronto — but for a brief but memorable time when they first arrived, the family had to move into the huge Royal York Hotel, the largest hotel in Toronto — in fact, the largest in Canada.

For Marilyn's mother and father, though, there was something even more important than finding a house. They wanted to find the right school for Marilyn. She had earned good marks at the LeMarchant School in Halifax, and her proud parents wanted her to continue her success. They decided to enroll her at St. Mary's Convent, which was a Catholic school. The decision wasn't made lightly. The Bell family had a Protestant background, not Catholic — and in those days in Toronto, matters of religion could be taken very seriously indeed by many people.

Marilyn's parents were inclined to put education ahead of religion, and St. Mary's had a reputation as one of the best schools in the entire city. Moving into a new school and making new friends is always hard, but even though she joined the school in mid-term, Marilyn passed her classes with first-class honours. She stayed at St. Mary's for that year and the next, then graduated to Loretto College School just a few blocks away — and there she continued to earn top marks.

But there was more to life for Marilyn than studying. From the very first day she arrived in Toronto Marilyn wanted to do something — something that would be fun, something active, something that would allow her to meet even more friends. Very soon she settled on the idea of swimming. The Oakwood Pool was nearby, so Marilyn joined the Dolphinette Club there.

That first summer in Toronto was a busy one for the Bell family as they settled into their new home. Marilyn's father was working hard at his new job, and it soon became obvious that the family wasn't going to be able to take any long holidays away from home that summer. Instead, they would take a holiday a day or two at a time right in the city. For Marilyn, who was nine years old that summer, that meant going swimming as much as she could. To make it easier, Marilyn's father bought her a season's ticket at the Oakwood Pool. It was expensive — a full $15 — but it allowed Marilyn to take 10 professional swimming lessons.

It was at Oakwood that Marilyn met Alex Duff, who

ran the Dolphinette Club and who was an exceptional swimming trainer. Alex had earned a reputation as a coach who trained champions. One of his swimming students, Evelyn Buchanan, was Canadian diving champion for several years, and Virginia Grant went on to become a member of Canada's swimming team at the British Empire and Commonwealth Games in Vancouver, British Columbia, in 1954.

Alex had many students to teach, however, so he rarely had time to give Marilyn any special attention. More than anything, he wanted to see that all his students learned the basics of the sport. Marilyn was a diligent student and developed a strong and confident swimming style, her own version of a classic crawl stroke.

Perhaps it was because he conducted all his classes at the Oakwood Pool and rarely ventured to the lake, but for some reason Alex seemed to favour sprint swimming more than long-distance racing. That wasn't a problem for Marilyn at first, but as she developed over the years, she realized she was better at long-distance swimming than the other girls. As time went by it would become more and more obvious that she was going to have to find another trainer. Sooner or later she would need someone who understood the particular training required by a swimmer whose races could last for many hours, not just a few seconds.

That's the Way to Swim, Kid!

That was all in the future, however; there was still much that Marilyn could learn from Alex and Oakwood. One very important lesson came during her second year with Oakwood. She entered her first long-distance race — it wasn't anywhere near as long as many of her later swims, but at the full distance of one mile (1,600 metres), the race at the Canadian National Exhibition was longer than any she had ever swum before. She was young, just 10 years old, but she had the enthusiastic support of her parents; in fact, her father had personally registered her name on the entry list for the race. The one-mile race was an important step in the young athlete's career. For one thing, it was the first time that the name of Marilyn Bell appeared in the printed program as a contestant in a public competition. But even more important, Marilyn would have a chance to meet some other people who were involved in swimming competitions. The race at the Ex would give her an inside look at the sport she enjoyed so much.

While it was her first big race, however, it was not one she would win. Even before the starting pistol was fired, Marilyn could see that this race would be hard. For one thing, many of the other girls in the race seemed to be much more confident. Many of them were from the Lakeshore Swimming Club, where all the swimmers regularly went swimming in Lake Ontario. As she stood there on the starting barge, looking out at the choppy water on the lake, Marilyn could only look and wonder how difficult it would be to swim in the tossing, turbulent waves.

Marilyn hadn't ever raced in the lake before. She'd prepared for the race by swimming from one end of the Oakwood Pool to the other, back and forth, back and forth, counting the laps until they added up to a mile. Not only was the water in the Oakwood Pool smooth and shallow, it was also heated — while the water in Lake Ontario was deep and could be downright chilly.

Whatever doubts or fears she might have had, Marilyn put them out of her mind. She splashed away with the rest of the racers when the starting gun was fired. The other swimmers were racing quickly ahead, while Marilyn seemed to be having trouble with the tossing waves. Still, she wouldn't let the cold water and the waves stop her. She maintained her pace, stroke after stroke after stroke.

As she approached the midway point, she saw all the others had already turned around and were well on their way back to the finish line. But she didn't give up. She kept on. Finally she reached the midway point and turned around, trying to keep up her pace — stroke, stroke, stroke. It was too much for her. She couldn't maintain her pace all the way. It was impossible. But still she kept swimming as fast as she could — stroke, stroke, stroke. She was getting tired. She wanted to quit. She wouldn't let herself quit. She couldn't quit. The waves and the water were too much. She needed a rest. So she gave herself a rest — the kind of rest that would carry her closer to the finish line. She rolled over and began to swim on her back — stroke, stroke, stroke — each stroke carrying her further along the course.

That's what did it for her — she coasted on her back and stroked her way to the end, and earned a small but heartfelt round of applause at the finish line. Marilyn came in last at ninth place with a time of one hour and 10 minutes, but she was a finisher. She was far from winning the Gold Medal for the race, but because she had gone all the way she won the respect of the other swimmers watching at the finish line.

As she climbed up the ladder out of the cold water, one of the older swimmers came over to Marilyn. She had a towel ready and wrapped it around Marilyn's shivering shoulders. Marilyn was glad about the towel, because she was chilled to the bone. But something the older swimmer said warmed Marilyn much more than any towel ever could. "That's the way to swim, kid!" she said. "Finish a race if you can!"

It was a surprising moment, a sudden unexpected experience that Marilyn would never forget, because the older swimmer who congratulated her was a well-known champion. Marilyn knew all about her. It was Winnie Roach Leuszler, the same swimming star who would compete against Marilyn and Florence Chadwick just a few years later in their famous race across Lake Ontario.

There was someone else that day that was impressed by Marilyn's swimming — Gus Ryder. The famous coach of the Lakeshore Swimming Club had noted her determination as she fought her way to the finish line in her first big race. Gus knew she was young, but he'd worked miracles with young swimmers before. That very afternoon Marilyn's father had a serious discussion with Gus about Marilyn and her swimming career. Syd Bell knew how disappointed his daughter was with her ninth-place showing, and he wondered if she might do better at Lakeshore than she was doing at Oakwood. Maybe there was something about Lakeshore and Gus that would be better for Marilyn. At Oakwood, after all, coach Alex Duff seemed to put the emphasis on sprint-racing. Could she do better with Gus at Lakeshore?

There was only one way to find out. Gus agreed that Marilyn could come to the Lakeshore Swimming Club.

As the club's name implied, when the Lakeshore

Swimming Club began, the members really did most of their swimming at the shore of Lake Ontario, and also in the Credit River. That was during the summer months. When it got too cold for outdoor swimming, the Club members would train at indoor pools, often at the school pool at Humberside Collegiate. It was there that Marilyn had her first session with the Lakeshore Swimming Club, and with Gus.

It was an important meeting for Marilyn. She quickly learned that Gus Ryder had a very different style of teaching. There was a shy side to Marilyn. When she was with the Dolphinette Club at the Oakwood Pool she never was one to push her way to the front of a swimming class to demand help from coach Alex Duff. She simply wasn't used to special attention of any kind, so she was surprised — and pleased — when the famous Gus Ryder himself got into the swimming pool to see her swim and analyze her stroke style.

Gus watched her carefully as she swam from one end to the other in the Humberside Collegiate pool. Then he told her to stop, and right there and then they had a serious talk about her swimming and what she wanted to do at the Lakeshore Swimming Club. Gus outlined what he thought she needed to work on, especially over the winter months before the club could return to the open waters of the lake and the river — and he made it clear that becoming a champion wouldn't just happen. She would have to put all her energy into it.

Gus spoke frankly, as he always did. "Marilyn," he said, "with plenty of hard work, rigid training and complete dedication to the job, there's no reason you can't be a fine distance-swimmer. Just forget about sprint-racing." Marilyn listened to every word — that was just the message she wanted to hear!

Very soon, the Lakeshore Swimming Club became Marilyn's second home. There were some days, especially in the summer, when it seemed she spent more time in her new swimsuit decorated with the Lakeshore crest than she did in regular clothes.

Marilyn was much more than an ordinary member of the club. She was more dedicated than most young members. She was still a junior, but Gus and some of the others were beginning to treat her like she was one of the seniors. The seniors were the serious swimmers, the ones who went for longer training swims down the Credit River and out into Lake Ontario. Gus would give them complicated training. On one swim they'd have to swim hard for a certain distance doing exactly 55 strokes a minute, then they'd have to speed up to 64 — Gus always had a strategy. Cliff Lumsden was the leader of the seniors, the one Gus trusted to lead the group on the long swims.

Cliff was the big star of the Lakeshore Swimming Club. He was a handsome and muscular 18-year-old when Marilyn first began swimming in the Credit River that summer. He was one of Gus's oldest students and had won just about every long-distance race around. Cliff was a champion.

Marilyn and the other serious swimmers would stand in a line in the river while Gus gave them their instructions. "Okay," Gus would yell, "take a sustained 55 down to the mouth, and step it up when you head into the lake." The group would get ready to start and Gus would pass on some final advice.

"And, Cliff," Gus would shout, "watch Marilyn. Don't overtire the kid, she thinks you hold her back!"

Marilyn was 11 years old that summer, still not the strongest swimmer, but she was making great progress. What really counted, she knew, was trying hard. It took commitment, dedication, determination — it took heart. That's what Gus said — it was the one of the biggest lessons he taught his swimming classes.

"I don't care how many muscles or brains you think you have," Gus told his students. "If you haven't the heart for distance racing, you might as well quit now."

Marilyn had heart. That's why she was here in the darkness swimming across Lake Ontario in the middle of the night. She was here for the challenge. She wasn't a quitter; she'd proved that at her first race at the CNE, and in dozens of club races afterwards. She didn't know where Florence Chadwick was any more — Florence and her guide boat had taken a different course long ago — but Marilyn knew she had to try to stay ahead. All she could see were the bobbing lights in the *Mipepa.* All she could hear was Gus calling out to her. "That's the girl, Marilyn," he said. "You're doing fine."

The lessons that Gus had taught her were second nature to her now. They were automatic, just like her steady stroke. She was still doing 64 a minute. She didn't need to count it out. She just knew. After all that training, she knew what 64 felt like. She kept it up — stroke, stroke, stroke.

Suddenly she felt something strange. Something was grabbing at her bathing suit! It was a lamprey eel! The horrid creature was a nasty little sea monster with a bloodsucking mouth. Lampreys were ugly. They could kill a fish.

Before the race began Marilyn had worried about being attacked by them. "If I find an eel on me," she said, "I'll scream!"

Now here it was, just a small lamprey that had attached itself to her swimsuit. But she didn't scream. Instead, she remembered what Gus said to do about eels. She grabbed the little lamprey firmly and pulled it off her suit. The eel was wriggling in her hand as she lifted it up above the waves. She tossed it away — just like Gus always said — and resumed her stroke, stroke, stroke.

Swimming in the dark wasn't all that hard, but it was lonely. When Marilyn first saw the *Mipepa*, the light at the back of the boat was the only one she could see. She asked Gus to turn on all the lights, so she could see more. That helped a bit, but she still couldn't see the faces of the people in the boat with Gus. She could hear their voices calling out to her, calling out in the darkness, but she couldn't see them. It would be nice to see their faces. It would be nice not to be so alone.

Chapter 3

There Was Always Someone Who Needed Help

Gus Ryder was used to winning. Marilyn Bell's race across Lake Ontario was the biggest and longest race he'd ever been involved in, but it certainly wasn't the first. Riding in the *Mipepa*, he was working almost as hard as Marilyn. He had a lot on his mind and had a lot to do. In front, way off in the distance, he could see a bright light shining through the gloomy night. It was the giant spotlight that the CNE had set up on a tall tower to guide Florence Chadwick and the other swimmers to the finish line at Exhibition Park. If he strained in the darkness, he could also see Marilyn swimming alongside the *Mipepa*, though not well — unless he shone his flashlight on her. But even in darkness he could see her white swimming cap bobbing as she stroked her way through the waves.

He checked her stroke. Marilyn had been in the water for a couple of hours now and she was in great shape. She had learned her lessons well. There was no doubt of it — Marilyn had turned out to be another one of his star students. Helping young athletes achieve their goals was nothing new to Gus Ryder, though. The habit was part of his life long before he started the Lakeshore Swimming Club.

As long as Gus could remember he'd been pitching in, helping out, and "playing the game," whatever the game might be. Gus was a born sportsman, and a born leader. Back in his own youth, when he was Marilyn's age and even younger, he knew every rink and playing field in Toronto. He was always on the team, no matter what sport he and his pals decided to play. "Anything that involved a ball, a puck, a net, or even a wall," Gus would say, "became, for the moment, my favourite game."

Gus was a strong competitor in rowing races. In baseball, he pulled on the catcher's mask and played behind the bat. He played defence in hockey and in his teens was good enough to make the roster of the acclaimed CNR-Express team. He was even picked for the Ravina League's All-Star team for a special game against the Varsity Grads, renowned as one of the very best hockey teams in all of Canada — which, in those days, meant it was one of the best in the world. The Grads were famous for trouncing their opponents, and many of the Ravina fans had few doubts that the All-Stars would soon join the long list of teams that the Grads quickly defeated. But Gus and the other All-Stars were made of stronger stuff. They all played harder than the Ravina fans, and the Grads, expected. The All-Stars didn't know how to play to lose; they played to win. The Grads, however, were as powerful as ever. It was a hard-fought match that ended in a tie. So Gus and the All-Stars didn't win, but neither did they lose. And considering that they were playing against the mighty Varsity Grads, earning a tie was regarded by many as being worth just about as much as an outright victory.

Gus always enjoyed swimming and diving, but one winter day when he was 18 he learned a lesson about water that would change his life. It happened in the midst of a game of scrub hockey on Grenadier Pond in High Park in Toronto's West End. It wasn't a real game. The ice on the famous pond was far too rough and bumpy for serious play, but it was good enough for a bunch of players enjoying an afternoon on the ice.

Suddenly, two players who had been scuffling for the puck cried out in alarm. The ice cracked beneath them, and the boys splashed down into 30 feet of freezing water. Many of the players who saw the boys fall in stood there stunned, not knowing what to do, and not moving at all — as if they were frozen to the ice. But Gus wasted no time. He yelled to the other players: "The pike poles! Get the pike poles!" Someone dashed to fetch the life-saving poles from the shore of the pond, and Gus started on his way to edge of the hole in the ice, where the two players were flailing in the water and grabbing at the ice, trying to hang on. Gus slid out on his belly, spreading his weight as widely as he could across the crumbling ice. Someone passed him a pole. He pushed it forward to the boys in the pond.

"Grab hold of this!" Gus yelled. Finally, one boy grabbed the pole and did as he was told. He managed to grasp the pole and crawl out of the deadly hole in the ice. Moments later, the second boy tried to follow. Gus had a firm hand on the pole to steady it. He could feel it twist slightly in his hand as the boy tried to crawl out of the hole. Then Gus felt the pole snap! The boy, halfway out of the water, tumbled back into the frigid water.

Gus rushed closer to the edge, sliding right up to the brink. He managed to reach under the arms of the scared boy. Two other rescuers were at his side. Gus lifted the boy up, and the others managed to drag him back to safety.

That left Gus all alone out on the ice at the crumbling edge of the hole. He twisted around to get away from the treacherous icy water, but the ice was too weak to bear his weight any longer. In an instant the ice cracked and Gus was dumped face first into the pond. He fell into the cold, silent world beneath the ice and felt the tremendous shock of the freezing water. Down, down, down he sank in the pond. He twisted and kicked and waved his arms, and slowly began to rise. But when he got all the way to the top, he was still underwater and unable to breathe. Gus was trapped beneath the ice!

In the awesome quiet below the ice Gus could hear one clear voice. It was his own voice. He was telling himself not to panic, but to be calm. "Think!"

Gus took command of himself and began giving himself orders, just as he had given orders to the two boys who fell in, orders that had saved their lives. Now he must save his own life. He told himself to open his eyes. He tried to see his hands, and saw they were pressing against the ice above his head. His head had banged on the ice when he came up, and his neck was bent at an uncomfortable angle. He tried to straighten up and look around to see if he could find the hole he fell in.

He turned and twisted until he saw a bright shaft of light slanting through the dark waters — there it was, the hole. He pushed himself along until he saw nothing above but open sunshine. He pushed his face into the daylight and filled his aching lungs with fresh air.

In an instant, strong hands reached out and pulled him onto the ice and away from danger. Someone took off a coat and wrapped Gus up in it to help keep him warm. There was no one to give him first aid. There was no paramedic and no ambulance to take him to the nearest hospital. Life was much simpler, and much more risky, when Gus was young. He was soaked to the skin and chilled to the bone, but otherwise he was none the worse for wear after his death-defying adventure under the ice. He simply walked home in the borrowed coat.

Yet something happened as he walked home that would change his life. As he strode along the snowy path through High Park he kept thinking about the meaning of life and how he had been spared. Somehow, at that very moment in the park, 18-year-old Gus Ryder made a decision to learn everything he could about swimming, and everything about life-saving. It was almost as if he had given himself another order. It was a big order, one that he couldn't complete all at once, but it was an order that would guide his actions to the end of his days.

As if to reinforce that decision, Gus Ryder had another terrifying experience with water a few years later. The youth had grown into a young man. He decided to spend a summer prospecting in northern Ontario

— there was a bit of a boom in the mining industry and newspapers were full of stories of instant fortunes being made. Gus was drawn to the Red Lake district, a land of great mineral wealth as well as spectacular beauty.

One day, he and a buddy were paddling down a stream when they came on some rapids. They had only an instant to make up their minds — they could paddle quickly to shore and portage around the rapids, or they could try and ride through the rough water.

They were young and strong, but the stream was too wild for them. Their boat was heavy and hard to steer. The current caught them and the boat slumped into a deep trough. In an instant the boat was pitched over and the two men were tossed into the raging water. Gus was thrown deep. When he wrestled his head above the surface of the stream, he gasped for air. He felt like he was imprisoned in his heavy, waterlogged clothing. Once again he heard that voice in his head, his own voice commanding himself: "Think!"

Somehow he did it. He stayed calm and worked his way through the current and the rocks to the quieter waters along the banks of the stream. He pulled himself up onto dry land. He looked around to see his friend, but there was no sign. The man had been grasped by the power of the current and was swept to his death. It was a hard way for Gus to learn that lesson again — water could be the source of so much pleasure, for swimming and diving and boating, but it could also be deadly dangerous.

Even at carefully supervised swimming events, there was always the threat of danger. In 1927, three years before he started the Lakeshore Swimming Club, Gus was in a crowd of spectators at a swimming race at the CNE — it was the first great swimming marathon at the Ex and had attracted international attention. The strongest swimmer in the race was Ernst Vierkoetter, who had been nicknamed "the Black Shark of Germany." Shark or not, Vierkoetter was well in the lead in the race, which was being held along the long concrete breakwater by the lakeshore.

All along the breakwater were groups of spectators watching the swimmers as they swam lap after lap of the marathon. There were so many good swimmers to watch. Vierkoetter and the racers close behind him made it look so easy, but not everyone was doing as well in the cold waters of Lake Ontario.

There were two swimmers in particular who seemed to be having difficulty. The spectators on the breakwater could see them gasping for air, their arms splashing into the water uselessly, unable to get to the pace boats.

Then, shockingly, one of the men waved weakly

and then dropped beneath the surface of the lake. The spectators stood stock-still, simply staring in disbelief, unable to act. Only one man pushed through the crowd to the edge of the breakwater. He tore off his jacket and dived in — that man was Gus Ryder.

Gus swam directly to the place where the man had been and found him sinking down. He grabbed the swimmer's hair and pulled him to the surface, up so the drowning man could get some air into his lungs.

The swimmer was hard to handle. He had coated his body with a thick coat of grease in an attempt to stave off the cold. Still, Gus pulled and pushed the man over to the edge of the breakwater. The other spectators were waiting there to pull the swimmer to safety.

They got him up, and Gus was about to come out himself when he heard another man yell.

"There goes the other one!"

Gus turned and saw a frail wave from the other swimmer as he too sank lower and lower into the waves. Once again, Gus swam to the rescue. Once again, he had to wrestle with the body of a swimmer coated with grease, but once again he brought a drowning man to safety.

Later, when they were all wrapped in blankets to keep warm, a doctor revealed the mystery of why the two men had both stopped so suddenly. The heavy grease they used had completely blocked the pores of their skin. In effect, the two swimmers were literally suffocating in the water. Gus learned a valuable lesson that day — he would never recommend that swimmers should use grease in cold water.

Gus never thought of himself as a hero, but once again he had proven what a difference it meant to act quickly when someone got in trouble in the water. It was part of the lessons he gave every student.

"Every year," he said, "many people drown because other swimmers standing nearby become fascinated by the actions of the drowning victim."

The person having difficulties doesn't always look like they're in trouble, Gus explained. Anyone nearby who fails to recognize the signs of distress can be "stunned into inactivity."

All too often, he said, "the would-be rescuers delay, until too late." Without instant action, "the victim is gone."

Gus eventually was able to follow that private order he made to himself, and put into practice his determination that everyone who went into the water to swim would also come out again, safe and sound. Gus had other responsibilities, of course. He launched his own business operating a customs brokerage in 1930 — which was an act of great bravery at the time, considering that the Depression had devastated the economy. That wasn't the only important step Gus took — 1930 was also the year that Gus married his sweetheart, Phyllis Hamilton. Gus and Phyllis were made for one another. She would forever support her husband's passion for water sports and safety.

Even with all his business concerns, Gus still found time for swimming. He became a part-time lifeguard at the beach on Lake Ontario. At the time Gus and his bride were living in New Toronto, the quiet suburb on the western edge of Toronto that later became part of the big city. Not far from his home was Lake Ontario, and just as appealing, the lower stretches of the Credit River. For most lifeguards, the job was easy. They could simply stay on the beach and keep an eye on the young kids playing in the waves. Not Gus, though — he wasn't content to just watch. He wanted to get involved. He began giving swimming lessons, free of charge, right there on the lakeshore to anyone who looked like they needed a bit of instruction — and there was always someone there who could do with a bit of help.

In no time at all, the lakeshore swimming classes became the Lakeshore Swimming Club. There was clearly a need. As the Depression continued, the free swimming in the lake was a prime source of recreation for thousands of young Toronto boys and girls, as well as grown men and women — and Gus wanted to make sure they could all enjoy swimming there safely.

Gus was a wonderful teacher. He knew how to give his students confidence. He taught them to trust themselves in the water. He showed them how to float, how to keep their legs straight and kick, how to breathe, and how to stroke. He had perfected what was called the "windmill" stroke, which combined what Gus regarded as the best elements of the three major styles of swimming at the time: the Australian, American, and Japanese. He took the rolling shoulder motion of the Australian crawl, and added the powerful flutter kick of the American style. To this, he added the Japanese emphasis on physical condition — on this point, Gus was adamant.

"If you are not in condition, it doesn't matter what stroke you use," Gus told his students. "If you are not in condition, you might as well try to dog-paddle your way up Niagara Falls!"

But teaching the strokes and kicks wasn't enough for Gus. It wasn't enough for his students just to know how to swim, how to avoid getting into trouble in the water, and how to get back to shore safely. Gus insisted that all his students had to know how to help someone else who needed it, and help them right away. That same summer of 1930 Gus came up with a slogan that would crystallize his philosophy: "Everyone a life-saver!"

Gus was serious about it. From the very beginning, lessons in how to save lives were part of the classes at the Lakeshore Swimming Club. Along with the drills for speed-swimming, and the endless practices for the long-distance swimmers, Gus always included sessions for life-saving. There were drills and demonstrations. "If you can't save lives in the water," Gus declared time and again, "you'll never swim for Lakeshore."

The club took on a life of its own. Older students became senior instructors, teaching the younger students. Being a member of the Lakeshore Swimming Club for a year or two became part of growing up for hundreds of boys and girls in the western end of Toronto. With no permanent home the club was often on the move. During the cold months, the club members would travel to whichever pool Gus had found to accommodate them — sometimes it was a pool at a school, and other times they'd gather at the West End YMCA. And when summer came they knew they'd usually be down at the shores of Lake Ontario or the banks of the Credit River.

For some students, it wasn't always easy to get from their homes to the pool where Gus was going to be holding classes, so there were times when Gus would offer yet another lesson — if his students couldn't get to him, he would go to them. In those days Gus had an old Ford automobile, a car that always had room for one more passenger. On his way driving to the pool Gus would stop and pick up any of his students who needed a ride — and with one particular class of junior boys, it seemed they all did, all the time.

Cliff Lumsden, who was one of the longest-serving members of the club, had a favourite memory of the time Gus picked up a total of 16 young boys and took them to the West End Y.

It was quite the sight — the first ones into the car got to sit on the seats, while the rest had to wriggle in and sit or stand the best they could. There were even four boys loaded in the open trunk of the car. Laughing and shouting they travelled to the Y, looking almost like they were a stray part of a circus parade.

The boys had their one-hour swimming class, followed by a noisy 15 minutes of free time to splash and play, then the raucous gang crowded back into the car with Gus.

On their way back heading home, Gus made a wee detour and stopped at a popular ice cream stand. He placed his order, no doubt the biggest order of the day: "Seventeen double-dip ice cream cones, please." Then the popular swim coach and his happy students, contented and finally quiet, could continue on their way.

But Gus knew there was more to coaching than sweet treats and gentle words of praise. There were times he was not above playing a little trick on his students — like the stunt he pulled on Cliff Lumsden. When Cliff was getting ready to compete in the 1949 Marathon at the CNE, a 24-kilometre race, he naturally asked Gus to help him train for the big event. Gus agreed.

The training took many weeks, but there was one Sunday morning session that Cliff would never forget. Cliff and Gus got down to a long concrete breakwater along the water's edge, where Gus could walk on a solid concrete pier while Cliff was swimming alongside. It was the perfect place for a long-distance swimmer to practice.

It was early in the morning, about 10 minutes to 7 a.m., when Cliff dived in. As soon as he hit the water Cliff almost jumped back out.

"Gus," he yelled, "the water's freezing! Brrrr!

"I could never last in this ice water! I'm getting out!"

Gus just looked at him and waved his hand for silence.

"What do you mean you're getting out?" Gus said. "Why, the water is warm as toast. Look."

As he spoke, Gus bent down and dipped a thermometer into the water. He held it there as Cliff looked on in amazement, and in silence.

Cliff watched Gus pull the thermometer out. Gus stood tall and held the thermometer up to read the temperature. "See what I mean, Cliff? — why, it's warm water, for you," Gus said. "Look," he said, flashing the thermometer in front of Cliff's eyes, "it's 63 degrees."

Gus had a Fahrenheit thermometer — 63 degrees was a shade more than 17 degrees Celsius, cool but comfortable.

Cliff didn't get a good look at the thermometer, and he still felt cold, but he started his long practice swim anyway. Gus marched beside him, shouting encouragement from time to time, as Cliff swam from end to end along the breakwater.

Gus kept track of the laps as Cliff swam out the miles — two miles, five miles, then eight and 10, and finally 15. Cliff was cold and tired. He'd been in the water for hours. "Gus," he called out, "don't you think this is enough for today?"

Gus stopped but didn't answer right away. "I'll tell you what, Cliff," he said, "just swim two more miles and we'll call it a day."

Cliff was ready to get out right away. He didn't want to swim two more miles. "How about settling for one mile, Gus?"

Gus agreed, and Cliff set off to do one final mile. When he was done, Cliff slowly climbed out. He felt colder than he'd ever been in his life.

"Gus," he said, "no kidding, is that water 63?"

Gus was quick to answer. "If you don't believe me," he said, "look for yourself." He handed the thermometer to Cliff.

Cliff dipped the thermometer again and checked it — this time, with his own eyes.

"I was right!" he exclaimed. "That water's only 53 degrees!" That was a far cry from what Gus said it was — 53 degrees was less than 12 degrees Celsius. No question about it, 53 degrees was darn cold!

Cliff stood there, speechless and trembling with the cold. Gus leaned over and had a look at the thermometer in Cliff's shivering hand.

"Stop jiggling," Gus said. He had another look at the thermometer.

"Hmmm," Gus said. "I did make a mistake at that, Cliff. It's my eyes, I guess."

That wasn't the only time that Gus had pulled a little trick on a student — not by a long shot. He did it because he knew he had to. When he fooled Cliff into staying in the cold water that Sunday morning, he gave Cliff a lesson that was to prove invaluable to him — Cliff learned he really could swim in cold water. On the day the Men's Fifteen-Mile Marathon was held at the CNE, Cliff had to compete against 84 other swimmers. The race had attracted all the best racers, all of them in top condition — but not all of them were as used to cold water as Cliff was.

The lake was colder then than it had been for years — just 51 degrees (10.5 degrees Celsius). Into the frigid water, 85 men dived in at the start of the race, but it wasn't long before one decided to get out because the water was too cold. Then another got out, and another — then dozens more, all because they couldn't stand to swim in the cold water. After a while there were only three men left, and Cliff Lumsden was in the lead. He never looked back. He led all the way. Cliff won the race and won the Grand Prize of $5500, plus a $50 bonus prize for each of the 15 mile-long laps, and another $50 for swimming the fastest mile in the race.

That day Cliff Lumsden proved he was a champion swimmer — but he also proved that Gus Ryder was a champion coach.

Now, in the darkness out on Lake Ontario with Marilyn Bell, Gus was working his strategy over in his mind. He knew there were some little tricks he'd need to play on her. There were some things he'd have to tell Marilyn to encourage her and some things that she wouldn't need to know right away. He hadn't bothered to tell Marilyn how Florence Chadwick was doing, for instance. Marilyn was down in the waves and couldn't see when Florence's boat disappeared off in another direction. Gus knew Marilyn had to rely on him for news about the race — and it didn't seem right to interrupt her with things she didn't need to know when she was swimming along so well. He'd save the good news, whatever it might be, for when it would make the most difference. Gus would always wait for the right moment to tell a swimmer something and always present a message in the best way possible. It was all part of coaching. It was all part of winning.

Chapter 4
I Wanted to Quit

The end to Marilyn Bell's swim across Lake Ontario came early. The race was over. Marilyn was too tired to go on. She was exhausted and ached all over. Another lamprey eel had come nibbling at her and had tried to fasten itself to her thigh. She pulled it off and threw it away, just like the first one. Then another one came, and another, and another. She hated them. Marilyn had been in the water for just four hours, but for most of the past 30 minutes she had to fight against waves that were as much as 12 feet high. She was swimming into the main part of the current from the Niagara River as it swept into Lake Ontario. It was even a challenge for Jack

Russell, who was operating the *Mipepa*, to navigate through the heaving mountains of water. Marilyn was worn out. She stopped swimming. She called out to Gus.

"I'm cold," she called out. "I'm numb." She didn't need to tell anyone she was tired. Florence Chadwick had been able to sleep as long as she wanted on the day before the race started, because only she knew when the race would start; her exclusive contract with the CNE gave the undisputed power to decide. Marilyn had been up all day wondering when, and if, Florence would ever make up her mind — and now she'd been up almost all night. Now Marilyn was tired, cold, and miserable.

If there was anyone who could help Marilyn now it was Gus. He always seemed to know what a swimmer needed to hear — he brought out the best in people. Lakeshore had its stars, like Cliff Lumsden, but Gus wouldn't allow the club to cater strictly to the needs of a few pampered stars. Cliff was a Lakeshore instructor and spent many hours helping to teach younger students.

And as she became a stronger, more experienced swimmer, Marilyn had become an instructor too.

No, at Lakeshore stars weren't pampered. They were put to work helping the younger swimmers — and no one was ever turned away who wanted to learn to swim. It was a fundamental part of Gus Ryder's sense of mission. "Champions may come and go," he said, "but kids go on forever."

And not only kids came to learn. The oldest member of the Lakeshore Swimming Club was an 80-year-old woman who'd heard about the swimming lessons. "I guess you'll think I'm pretty old to want to learn to swim, Mr. Ryder," she said. "But, well, I never had the opportunity before," she explained. And given the opportunity, she soon learned.

The very youngest student was so young he earned a degree of fame in his day. One day Dr. R. C. Hughes, another resident of New Toronto, came to Gus with his twin sons, who were then just three years old, and asked if they could be taught to swim. In a few short weeks, the twins were swimming with all the confidence of children many times their age.

Then, one afternoon when Dr. Hughes had called by to pick up the twins after their lesson, he showed Gus the newest addition to the family, wee Davie Hughes, a sturdy 14-month-old.

"How about teaching *this* boy to swim now, Gus?" he said. He meant it as a joke. But it wasn't a joke to Gus Ryder.

"Okay, Doctor," Gus said. "Take off his clothes and pass him right down to me."

Dr. Hughes hardly knew what to say. It took him a

moment to realize that Gus was serious. But in just a minute or two, young Davie was in the pool with Gus, taking his first swim riding on Gus's back and holding on to his neck.

After that, there was no stopping him. Young Davie Hughes was a fast learner — and a fast swimmer too. In three months he could swim across the width of the pool. A few weeks later he could swim the length of the pool from one end to the other.

Davie Hughes wasn't even two years old and he could swim with a strong confident stroke. He was the darling of the Lakeshore Swimming Club. It was easy for the instructors to encourage new students when everyone could see how easy it was to learn to swim — why, even a tiny kid could do it!

Davie became a celebrity. When the officials at the CNE heard about him, they wanted the young lad to put on a demonstration at the Ex. Davie did it the year he turned two, agreeing to swim a distance of half a mile (eight hundred metres). He did it perfectly, his short arms maintaining a perfect stroke, and his legs doing a perfect flutter kick. He was an excellent student. The first time he did his show at the Ex, he was presented with a special trophy by CNE Sports Director George Duthie.

Several reporters cornered Gus after Davie's

demonstration, demanding details about the young swimmer.

"Gentlemen," said Gus, "you may think that the boy is an amateur, but believe me, he's a full professional." And in fact, the CNE paid Davie a small sum for every time he swam.

As years went by, Davie Hughes grew older and was no longer such a novelty attraction. He was just another dedicated member at the Lakeshore Swimming Club.

At the Lakeshore Swimming Club, Gus had even taught children to swim who were not able to walk without assistance. Children whose young bodies had been badly damaged by disease or accidents were always welcome at Lakeshore.

It started simply enough. One day Gus met a mother and father who were members of the Parents' Cerebral Palsy Association. They had just one question for Gus: did he think he could teach children with cerebral palsy to swim?

Gus pondered the question for a moment. "Yes," he said. "I do think I can teach those kiddies to swim. Just give me a day or so to get my theories in order — then bring them on. We'll look after them."

No other swim club in Toronto, and no other coach, had ever welcomed so many students with severe physical disabilities. It didn't matter what sort of challenge the students faced — whether they were blind or deaf, or had cerebral palsy or polio, or had been badly crippled in a car crash — Gus resolved to find a way to teach each of them to swim.

"We're teaching these youngsters to swim," Gus declared, "so that by doing so, the kids can help themselves."

Perhaps the special care and attention that was required would be too much for most clubs, too much for most coaches — but it certainly wasn't too much for Lakeshore, and certainly not for Gus Ryder. For Gus, the question went straight to his spiritual core. When he explained his philosophy to the Lakeshore instructors, and to anyone else who would listen, he recalled the teachings of the Bible. "Let us remember one last thing," he said. "When Christ said, 'Suffer little children to come unto me,' He meant crippled youngsters as well."

They came with canes and they came with crutches. They had braces on their legs or were brought to pool in wheelchairs. But once they got in the water, they were just kids who needed to be taught how they could have fun in the pool, and have fun safely.

It didn't take long for Gus to modify his teaching style to match the needs of his new students. Special days were assigned for students with similar challenges. He started with the students that he judged would be

easiest for the instructors to teach. That helped everyone gain confidence in the program. The young children
who always had to sit on the sidelines before were now
centre stage in the pool — happily splashing and swimming. The first ones who learned to swim became an
inspiration to all the rest still waiting their turn to join
the fun. At the same time, the Lakeshore instructors
were gaining valuable experience and learning that
these new students needed to be taught in ways that
were appropriate to their abilities.

For instance, students who were blind needed to
be told what water really is like. Students who had damaged arms or legs had one advantage; at least they could
see the water and watch the waves. But a blind youngster couldn't — and what they couldn't see, many would
fear. "When starting out to teach a blind youngster, or
adult, to swim," Gus said, "we must first of all, as
instructors, help the pupil to control the imagination."

Gus Ryder was an inspiration to every student he
encountered in the water. He had a similar influence on
people he met on dry land. When Gus presented his
sense of mission, he made people want to help him. He
found ways for other organizations to help the children
who came to the Lakeshore Swimming Club. Gus
became active in the Red Cross Society and soon was
the chairman of the Lakeshore Red Cross — he

managed to link the goals of the two organizations for a common cause, launching a vast "Learn to Swim" campaign in 1946. Literally thousands of children answered the call and joined in to learn to swim safely.

Gus found other willing supporters in the New Toronto community and elsewhere who admired his determination and would do what they could to help. That's how the Lakeshore Swimming Club finally got a permanent home.

Swimming in the lake was fine in the early days of the club during the Depression — and swimming in other pools was all right while the club was becoming established. But if the Lakeshore Swimming Club was going to grow and help more and more children, it was going to need proper facilities. After years of effort, it happened in 1952 when the club moved permanently to the new War Memorial swimming pool in New Toronto.

It would not have happened if it hadn't been for the efforts of hundreds of people who were inspired by one man, the coach of the Lakeshore Swimming Club. It would not have happened if not for Gus Ryder.

For Gus, every student was different, but all students had strengths they didn't know they had. It was his duty to help them find that strength, and help them put it to work.

Now, shouting out in the darkness from a boat in

the middle of Lake Ontario, he had to help Marilyn find her strength. She was aching. She was cold. She was ready to quit.

Trying to inspire Marilyn now was harder than teaching any of the thousand other members of the Lakeshore Swimming Club. They *wanted* to swim, but Marilyn wanted to stop. At the same time, she didn't want to disappoint Gus.

"Marilyn, you've swum all night, and that's really great," Gus shouted. "If you can do that you can do the rest," he said. "In another hour the sun will come up and it will be really nice."

But those cheering words made no difference. Marilyn didn't move. She stayed stopped. The others in the *Mipepa*, especially George and young Peter joined in, trying to encourage her, trying to make her feel she wasn't so all alone and cold in the middle of the lake.

"Come on, Marilyn," they shouted. "That's the girl!"

"Remember the little crippled kids at the Lakeshore."

"They're all cheering for you."

There was no response from the little girl bobbing about in the waves.

"Marilyn — give one more try for the Lakeshore kids."

Still only silence from the swimmer.

Gus didn't say anything else. He didn't offer to pull her into the boat. He didn't congratulate her on a fine attempt and tell her to stop now.

Instead, he pulled out the stick.

The stick had a small wire hoop on the end that could hold a paper cup. Gus got out a bottle of corn syrup and poured some into the cup on the stick, then held it out over the waves where Marilyn could reach it.

Marilyn knew about corn syrup. Everyone at the Lakeshore Swimming Club knew about corn syrup. In fact, every single person who lived in New Toronto knew about corn syrup. You certainly couldn't swim in the Credit River without knowing about the factory right there at Port Credit where they made Bee Hive Corn Syrup. Port Credit was famous across the country for corn syrup. Everyone knew corn syrup was energy food — and right now, Marilyn certainly was in need of a burst of energy.

She took the cup and brought it to her lips and sipped at the corn syrup. She was treading water. She was trying not to cry. Her eyes were wet and it wasn't all lake water.

Marilyn and Gus stared at one another in the gloomy night as she continued to sip at the syrup. Marilyn said nothing. Gus said nothing. There was nothing to say.

After an endless moment, Marilyn let go of the cup and it floated away. She put her head down and started swimming again.

Marilyn Bell was swimming for the Lakeshore kids. She was swimming for Gus Ryder. She was swimming for herself.

Dawn came, just like Gus said it would. The sun was up, but the day was not "really nice," not by a long shot. Marilyn had already swum a very long race. She was 22 kilometres out into the lake. What's more, she was far ahead of Florence Chadwick.

Marilyn didn't know it at the time, but she had passed ahead of Florence in the darkness within the first hour of the swim less than five kilometres from the shore on the New York State side of the lake. Her starting strategy — get ahead early and stay ahead — had paid off. If she could keep it up, there's no way she could lose. All she had to do was keep going and she would beat Florence.

But Florence was no longer a contender. The famous swimming champion and movie star had been beaten by Lake Ontario. Florence was terribly sick — she too had been badly battered by the rolling waves. The waves made her nauseous and had given her one violent vomiting fit after another. Finally, after a dozen horrendous convulsions, there was nothing left in her stomach that she could spit out. Shortly before 6 a.m., as the sky was streaking with light from the rising sun — her trainers stopped and pulled Florence Chadwick into the guide boat. Gus heard about Florence's departure soon enough, but he didn't tell Marilyn right away. In true Gus Ryder style, he decided he should keep that momentous news to himself. He would tell Marilyn later, all in good time.

But now, as the sun was rising rapidly over the lake, this was not a good time. It most definitely was not a good time for Marilyn Bell. With the increasing sunlight there was no more guessing about how Marilyn was feeling. Everyone in the *Mipepa* could see it as plain as day.

Everyone — Gus, Jack, young Peter, and *Star* reporter George Bryant — were all shocked to see how exhausted Marilyn looked. They saw the slack look of the muscles in her face. They saw the glassy stare in her eyes.

Marilyn's mother and father, however, couldn't see how tired their daughter was. They were further away in the other boat that was crossing the lake with Marilyn, the *Mona IV*. It was much larger, a real lake yacht; on board with her parents were more *Star* reporters and photographers.

Marilyn's strong swimming style had collapsed. She couldn't kick with her legs any more. Her legs were useless. She dragged them behind her, flailing at the water with her arms.

Marilyn said nothing. It hurt too much to say anything. But later, after the ordeal was over, she described how she felt. "My arms were tired," Marilyn said. "My legs ached.

"My stomach hurt in one big awful pain and I couldn't get my breath.

"I wanted to quit.

"When it gets to your stomach, marathoners say, you're through."

Marilyn Bell was through — or so it seemed.

There was no mistaking the water streaming down Marilyn's cheeks. The flow of tears wouldn't stop. George the reporter saw them pouring down her face and felt tears swell up in his own eyes.

"If it had been my decision," George said afterwards, "I'd have got her out of there right then."

But it wasn't George's decision to make. The decision would be made by Marilyn Bell — and by Gus Ryder.

Gus got out the stick again and loaded up another paper cup of corn syrup. He passed it to Marilyn, but this time that energy would go to waste. Marilyn couldn't hold her hand still. She was shaking from the cold and exhaustion. She reached for the paper cup but her hand shook so much the cup and corn syrup tumbled into the lake.

Slowly, Gus got another paper cup and filled it — but this time not with corn syrup. Instead, he filled the cup with liniment. Gus told Marilyn to roll over on her back, and to rub the liniment on her legs. Marilyn did as she was told, the tears still streaming down her face. She rubbed both legs until all the liniment in the cup was gone. The tears never stopped.

Gus finally broke the silence.

"Swim over here, Marilyn," he said. "We'll take you out."

Again, Marilyn did as she was told. She began paddling over to the *Mipepa*. Gus watched her with a careful eye. He saw immediately that the liniment had worked exactly as he hoped it would. Marilyn was kicking now with her legs — not strongly, but she working harder than before she'd stopped.

Stroke by stroke, Marilyn was coming closer to the *Mipepa*. Gus kept watching her swim — stroke, stroke, stroke — and then he made up his mind.

Gus turned to Jack Russell.

"Pull away, Jack," he said softly. Jack eased the throttle up a notch or two and the boat began to pull ahead. Marilyn kept swimming along — stroke, stroke, stroke — and she kept crying. With every stroke the waves washed the tears from her face, but did nothing to stifle the sound of her sobbing.

Gus coaches Marilyn from the *Mipepa*

The sound of the schoolgirl's agony was enough to break George Bryant's heart. He looked at Gus.

"That's a bad sign," Gus said to George. "If she keeps on crying, I'll have to take her out."

But the boat kept moving forward, toward Toronto and the CNE. Marilyn was still crying, but she was still swimming — stroke, stroke, stroke.

It wasn't the first time Gus had tested a swimmer to discover the limits of endurance. At the Lakeshore

Swimming Club, he did it all the time.

Now he had to wonder when Marilyn would find her limit. She always seemed to be able to do more. The first time he saw her swim — the time she finished in last place at the CNE race — he was struck by her determination and agreed to have her come to Lakeshore.

She had become a much better swimmer at Lakeshore. When she returned to the CNE swimming course the next year to compete in the Junior Girls' One-Mile Swim again, she was much faster and stronger. She came in at sixth place — definitely an improvement.

She continued to get better throughout her second year at Lakeshore, and was in great shape when she entered the CNE race for the third time.

Gus had encouraged her, offering all the support he could, but making it clear that she was going to be the one who would have to do the hard work. "If you think you can win the race, Marilyn, I do too," he said.

"You've had the training," Gus said. "Your chances are good. It's up to you."

It was a race to remember. Marilyn stood ready on the starting barge with the other girls. When the starting gun was fired, they all dived in, making one big splash. Very quickly the fastest swimmers pulled to the lead, leaving the slower ones behind. This time, Marilyn was in the lead.

But she wasn't alone.

She wasn't the only girl from the Lakeshore Swimming Club, and she wasn't the only girl who had learned so much from Gus Ryder. Alanna Angus, another Lakeshore member, was there and swimming just as fast as Marilyn.

It was an astonishing sight. Marilyn and Alanna were swimming side by side, matching stroke for stroke. To the spectators, the two Lakeshore racers looked like a team, but each was swimming hard to beat the other.

All the other swimmers were far behind. This was a going to be a two-girl race. They pounded the water as they approached the finish barge. Closer and closer came the two swimmers.

Then one reached out to be first to touch the barge. It was Alanna. Marilyn was second.

Second was good. It was better than sixth, better than ninth. But second was second — it wasn't first. Even so, it was another great improvement.

Marilyn sometimes seemed to lack the "killer instinct" that other racing swimmers had. Gus and Cliff and all the other instructors at Lakeshore Swimming Club told her about it.

"You're too placid, Marilyn," they'd say. "You must get your competitive spirit fired up for a race." But mere words weren't ever going to change Marilyn. She had her own way of showing her strengths and abilities.

In 1951, when she was 13, Marilyn had another chance to show everyone. One more time she entered her name to be a contestant in the Junior Girls' One-Mile Swim. Then, just because she felt so confident, she also entered her name for the Senior Girls' event, competing for the Ross Gold Trophy.

Normally, entering two races like that wouldn't cause any unusual problems — but there never seemed to be anything normal or usual about the races at the CNE. This year the weather played another dirty trick on the swimmers. The lake was far too rough for racing according to the original schedule, so many events had to be cancelled. The races would be held whenever the weather would allow. As a result, Marilyn was surprised to discover that both the Junior and Senior races were to be held on the same afternoon.

The Senior race came first. When she dived in at the start, Marilyn was surrounded by older and stronger swimmers. She was definitely a Junior in the midst of Seniors — but she was an accomplished and well-trained swimmer, who had learned to swim from the best. Marilyn swam her way through the pack of swimmers on her way to the halfway barge. By the time she was at the half-mile point, there was only one other girl in front of her, Vivian King from Winnipeg.

Marilyn swam as hard as she could. She narrowed the distance that Vivian had put between them, but couldn't close the gap completely. Vivian reached the finish barge well ahead of Marilyn, but Marilyn came in a clear second — earning second place as a Junior in a Senior race for the Ross Gold Trophy was almost as good as coming in first.

However, standing there on the barge afterwards with a towel over her shoulders, Marilyn did not have much time to reflect on what she had just accomplished. She wasn't even completely dry from the race when she heard the announcement on the public address loudspeaker.

"Contestants," the loudspeaker blared, "take your places for the Junior Girls' Mile-Swim."

That was all there was to it. There was no time to bask in the glory of coming in second. There was no time to rest. There wasn't even time to dry. It was time get back in the water. It was time to swim a race.

No — it was time to win a race, to come in first!

Swimming so soon after the race with the Seniors would have tired some girls out, but it was just a warm-up session for Marilyn. Now in her second race of the day, she was with girls her own age in the Junior category.

Again the race started with one big splash as the Junior girls all hit the water at the same moment. And again Marilyn quickly pulled to the front of the thrashing mass of swimmers. She was strong and racing ahead to the half-mile turnaround, swimming steadily — stroke, stroke, stroke. Marilyn was in the lead, but once again she was not alone. Shirley Campbell, the champion from the Ontario town of Fergus, was just as strong. With Shirley pressing hard, Marilyn was in the midst of her second two-girl race of the day.

The two girls pounded the water furiously. There was just a short distance to go, no more than four hundred metres, with Marilyn in the lead and Shirley trailing close behind. Marilyn strained harder and harder, kicking harder, stroking harder — stroke, stroke, stroke — working hard to pull further ahead, closer and closer to the finish barge.

As she got closer the crowd began to roar — it was the first time she had really *felt* the power of the crowd's cheers. They were cheering for her!

The roar of the crowd seemed to give her extra strength as she battled her way to the finish barge — and to victory! She had won! She was a true Lakeshore champion!

Marilyn was a champion all right. After that first major victory at the CNE, she had one success after another. Now, however, she certainly didn't look like a champion — or sound like a champion — as she swam alongside the *Mipepa*, weeping as she swam. Gus had told George he'd have to pull Marilyn out of the water if she continued to cry, and he was true to his word.

Yes, if she kept crying, he'd pull her out and take her to shore. The race would be over. But Marilyn was starting to swim with renewed vigour. She was kicking with her legs after rubbing them with the liniment that Gus had given her. And as she swam, she ran out of tears. She stopped crying. The sobs fell silent.

So Gus didn't stop the boat to pull her out of the water. He let her keep swimming — stroke, stroke, stroke — each stroke bringing her closer to Toronto, closer to the finish at the CNE.

Chapter 5

Working Hard to Turn a Dream into a Reality

Gus Ryder still had some tricks up his sleeve. Now that Marilyn was swimming in full daylight, it was time to get out his blackboard. The board wasn't large, just big enough. Gus could write a few words on it that Marilyn could read as she swam along. Marilyn was doing well, keeping up a remarkable pace, often going as high as 64 strokes a minute — stroke, stroke, stroke. It was a fabulous effort.

Gus wrote a message on the blackboard for Marilyn that was certain to bring a smile to her face.

DON'T FORGET THE DANCE TOMORROW NIGHT!

Working Hard to Turn a Dream into a Reality

It was easier for Marilyn to read the messages on the board than it was for her to hear anything that Gus might yell. As the day wore on he wrote many messages for her. Gus called the messages "blackboard psychology."

By mid-morning, Gus noticed that Marilyn was slowing down. She no longer kept to that remarkable 64-a-minute pace. It was 10:30 a.m., time for a big message — one that would really make a difference.

In big letters he wrote the news he'd been saving for just the right moment — and the moment had come. It was a message both short and sweet.

FLO IS OUT.

Now Marilyn finally knew what everyone else had already known for hours. Marilyn had beaten Florence Chadwick, the world's greatest woman swimmer. Now her only opponent was Winnie Roach Leuszler. Marilyn didn't know where Winnie was. She might be close behind. She could even be a bit ahead. Marilyn picked up her pace and was doing a steady 55 — stroke, stroke, stroke.

But it couldn't continue. Marilyn couldn't keep up the grueling speed. She slowed down. Gus got out his blackboard again.

DON'T LET THE CRIPPLED KIDS DOWN, he wrote. It seemed to help — when she saw the message, Marilyn smiled and started to swim faster.

When she slowed again later, Gus wrote a simpler note: SWIM FOR ME. Once again, it worked — for a while.

Gus would try anything to help his swimmer. He'd coached her through her amateur years and seen her blossom as a professional. She'd joined the ranks of the professionals at Lakeshore two years earlier, during the swim meet at the CNE.

Marilyn swam as an amateur in her first race at the Ex in 1952. She won the Barker Trophy for winning the Amateur Women's One-Mile race. Two days later she "turned pro" to compete in the Women's Three-Mile Marathon (4.8 kilometres). She was just 14, one of 20 women to compete in the race — she came in fourth and collected a prize of $300!

After that, she seemed to improve every time she got in the water. The next year she entered again and finished third, to win $500 — a major amount of money. In every race she entered, Marilyn seemed to be faster, stronger, better.

She was looking forward to an even better result in 1954, but this was the year the CNE changed everything. The swimming competitions were eliminated; instead they'd come up with this crazy idea of hiring Florence Chadwick. When she first heard about the cancellation, Marilyn was disappointed, but then she remembered

Cliff Lumsden's plans.

She had an idea. She took it to Gus.

"Cliff is entering the Atlantic City Marathon, Gus," she said. Gus knew that, of course, and he was also probably expecting what Marilyn said next.

"Do you think I could go along?" she said

Of course, Marilyn didn't want to be just a spectator. She wanted to swim the marathon herself — at more than 41 kilometres, it would be the longest race she'd ever swum.

Did Gus think she could do it? Did she have a chance? Would he let her do it? She wanted to know.

Gus listened carefully, and then carefully answered. "That's 26 miles of ocean, Marilyn," Gus said. "You'll have to ask you mother and dad. It's not for me to say.

"As for you having a chance in the race, well — it's certainly worth a try."

That was a true Gus Ryder answer. He was always ready to help a swimmer — but all he could ever offer would be help.

"It has to be your idea, Marilyn," he said. "I'm only your coach and trainer. The swimming is up to you."

The marathon race at Atlantic City was several weeks away. Marilyn convinced her parents and began the rigorous training she needed for such a long race.

The Atlantic City swim was brand new, but it was

one of the most challenging races in the world. This year Atlantic City was celebrating its centennial, and the marathon was one of the most exciting events to mark the event. Thousands, even hundreds of thousands of spectators were expected to be there. It was a wonderful dream for any competitive swimmer to be there for the Centennial Marathon.

Cliff and Marilyn set to work to make that dream a reality. There was no way they could find an exact duplicate of the Atlantic City swimming conditions in Lake Ontario. They'd never find a spot that could match the powerful tides and currents of the Atlantic Ocean. And they knew that taking a mouthful of lake water was nothing to swallowing a load of salty seawater.

Cliff went to New Jersey to check out the course on the long July 1 weekend. He swam a few miles over the route the race would take, trying to discover the secrets of the tides and currents that he and Marilyn would encounter. The race for the Centennial Marathon was set to go around Absecon Island, which meant encircling Atlantic City itself.

There were wild variations in water temperatures at Atlantic City. In the shallow bay, the water could be very warm, almost like a big bathtub. But as the course shifted out into the open ocean to go around Absecon Island the temperature could drop like a rock. A swimmer had to be ready for the rapid change.

To prepare for the jolt, Cliff and Marilyn went out of their way to practice in places along the Credit River they previously had stayed away from. They swam through warm weedy patches off in the shallow areas along the river's edge. They'd feel the heat, then swim way out into the lake to duplicate that dramatic drop in temperatures. Day after day they swam, hour after hour after hour — stroke, stroke, stroke.

Finally, they were ready to travel to Atlantic City where they could practice in the bay and in the ocean. In mid-July the two swimmers flew down to the coast with Cliff's mother and Joan Cooke, who was going to be team manager in charge of training until Gus arrived later. Joan was another veteran member of the Lakeshore Swimming Club and a close friend of Marilyn's — and she was also Cliff's sweetheart. They rented a seaside cottage that became the headquarters of the Lakeshore Swimming Club in Atlantic City.

Training was hard work — Joan made sure of that. They were in the water at nine o'clock each morning, swimming behind the boat that Joan was rowing. She would lead them through running tides and swirling currents, then blow her whistle to signal them to turn around. Then she'd lead them back to the cottage for the hearty lunch that Cliff's mother had prepared. After a two-hour rest they were back at it, swimming until it was time for supper.

Joan would give the swimmers another brief break to digest the meal, then she'd grab her whistle again and lead them out to the water for yet another hour of training.

About the only people they saw were other swimmers. There was one swimmer in particular who caught Marilyn's eye, a handsome lifeguard named Joe DiLascio. It would have been nice to have more time to see Joe, but there weren't any idle hours for socializing. With Joan and her whistle, there was no question of changing the strict routine. Cliff and Marilyn kept up the pace until Gus arrived. He arrived just before "Swim Day." Gus was going to be in Marilyn's boat.

The weather was almost perfect the day the Centennial Marathon was held; the skies were slightly overcast, which held back the heat. For weeks the hot summer sun had warmed the bay at Atlantic City so the water there was 82 degrees — about 28 degrees Celsius — a great temperature for children splashing along the shore, but far too warm, far too tiring, for serious racing. Once they swam clear of the bay, though, the marathoners would have to deal with the brisk chill of the ocean, with a sudden drop down to 70 degrees (21 degrees Celsius). There was also a fresh breeze, invigorating but also a bit irritating because it whipped salt spray onto the goggles most of the swimmers wore.

Before the race began, Cliff needed to find a doctor. His right elbow, which had developed a painful calcium deposit, was hurting too much to bend. The doctor gave him some shots to relieve the pain; the elbow was just beginning to bend normally when the race began.

When the starter's gun fired, a full contingent of 40 swimmers began to churn through the salt water, including both Cliff and Marilyn. They weren't the only Canadians in the marathon, however. Tom Park of Hamilton, who had often competed against Cliff at the CNE, had also made the trip to Atlantic City to enter the race.

Tom Park was a strong swimmer and one of the first to break away from the pack. Tom soon became the clear leader, but close behind was Cliff. The two Canadian lads were far ahead of all the American swimmers — and they held their commanding position until the end. Cliff and Tom had turned the Centennial Marathon into a two-man race. And not far behind, passing many men along the way, was Marilyn.

Tom held the lead until the 16-kilometre mark, and then Cliff found the strength to pass his old opponent — and for many more kilometres he kept the lead. Then the race got tighter as Tom pulled up again. The contest came down to the last three kilometres, as the two men swam together, stroke for stroke. Then, just as they were approaching the finish, the tide pushed Cliff into some pilings along the course. He quickly regained his pace, but Tom had pushed ahead, crossing the finish line first with a time of nine hours, 21 minutes, and 42 seconds. Cliff crossed just a couple of minutes later.

The excitement didn't end when Tom and Cliff were through and had reached the finish.

All along the course a fresh round of cheering started as another champion came closer and closer to the end. There was a young girl from Canada, just 16 years old, who was surging ahead of most of the men in the race, and well ahead of all the other women. It was Marilyn Bell!

With her was Gus, in a boat with his stick, his paper cups, and a cargo of corn syrup, often mixed with Pablum baby food, which was easy to digest and full of energy. He also had his famous blackboard. He'd been scribbling messages to Marilyn all through the race. And when Marilyn heard the roar of the crowd up ahead when Tom and Cliff crossed the finish line, Gus had written a special message he knew would add a little zest to Marilyn's stroke — he wrote that Cliff had won!

Elated that Cliff, her friend and fellow club member had won, Marilyn picked up her pace. If she won in the women's division, that would mean two Lakeshore champions! It was a long, hard test of her endurance. As well as the sudden shifts in temperature, Marilyn had had to keep swimming strongly even though her face and body were stinging from the many jellyfish she'd swum into. She was too tired to smile, but she kept on. Finally, she crossed the line with a time of 10 hours, seven minutes, and two seconds — almost a half-hour behind Tom and Cliff!

Marilyn was the seventh swimmer to cross the finish line that day, but the first woman. Taking First Place in the women's division at the Atlantic City Centennial Marathon was Marilyn's first major win. She received a prize of $1150.

Once she got out of the water, it didn't take long before she found out that Gus had told her a big fib when he'd written that Cliff had won the race. Tom was really the winner. So there weren't two winners from the Lakeshore Swimming Club. There was just one — Marilyn Bell.

When she heard the news, her first reaction was purely emotional — she gave Cliff a big hug and burst into tears on his shoulder. Then she turned and gave Tom a kiss of victory!

In Atlantic City, Marilyn had proven to Gus — and to the world — that she was a remarkable swimmer, despite her young age. She was a champion who could battle against the ocean waves for more than 10 hours and keep right on — stroke, stroke, stroke — until the end.

But now, here bobbing in the waves of Lake Ontario, there was little sign of that champion. Instead, all Gus could see was only the tired schoolgirl. The chorus of encouragement continued from Gus and George and young Peter.

"Marilyn!" they shouted.

"Marilyn! Keep fighting!"

"Don't stop!"

"Remember the crippled kids!"

Marilyn wasn't the only tired swimmer in the lake. Winnie Roach Leuszler had taken another route across the lake, but she had run into the same problems — the violent waves, the lamprey eels, and, most of all, the exhaustion. Winnie was a strong and experienced swimmer. She'd been the first Canadian woman to swim across the English Channel. But she wasn't going to be the first to swim across Lake Ontario. The lake had beaten her, just as it had beaten Florence Chadwick. At about the three-quarter mark, she was seized by a series of cramps that made it impossible for her to continue. She was in such pain she could hardly stay afloat. Her trainers reached down and pulled her from the torment of the waves. Now Winnie was out. Florence Chadwick was out. Marilyn Bell was all alone.

But Marilyn wouldn't celebrate this unexpected twist of events. By this time she'd been in the water for 17 hours straight — and she had now gone a total of 31 hours without sleep. During the Centennial Marathon at Atlantic City, she'd hummed to herself to break the monotony. She hummed the tune to "O Canada," and she hummed a popular song, "The Happy Wanderer."

Once the song got going in her mind it seemed to stay there forever. "I love to go a-wandering" — she would hum the tune and hear the words in her mind — "along the mountain track."

But there was no energy left now for humming. All she wanted to do was sleep — and sleep she did, even as she battled the waves of Lake Ontario.

"Marilyn!" shouted Gus, when he saw her falter. "Marilyn!" He held up his blackboard with another message he was sure would wake her up — $7500 IF YOU FINISH.

Marilyn was too sleepy to read it properly. To her tired eyes, it seemed to say $750, not $7500.

Even so, it cheered her up. She was back swimming. "I'll split it with you, Gus!" she yelled back.

This time it was true — for once Gus wasn't stretching the truth on his blackboard. While Marilyn had been swimming all alone through the tossing waves on Lake Ontario, there had been plenty of action back on the shore. For one thing, people had been gathering along the shoreline trying to catch a glimpse of her. People in the tall buildings in downtown Toronto, especially at the Royal York Hotel, kept checking out the windows, straining to see if they could catch sight of the growing number of boats that were accompanying her.

All the radio stations were talking about her on their news broadcasts, and some would interrupt their regular programs to pass on special reports from the lakeshore or from boats on the lake. The newspapers had published special editions. The reporters had besieged the administration offices at the CNE. Now that Florence and Winnie were out, they wanted to know, would Marilyn get the prize money?

The answer didn't come quickly — and it changed from hour to hour. At first, when Winnie was still in the race, the president of the CNE, Robert Saunders, declared that anyone who managed to complete the swim would get "a substantial amount of money." The sum grew as the hours ticked by — for a while, it was going to be $1000, then it became $5000. Now the prize money was $7500 — hour by hour the prize got bigger, and it was waiting for Marilyn.

But, in the end, no sum of money could help

Marilyn now. Her stroke was weak, and her legs had stopped moving again. She needed something that money could never buy. She got it from her best friend, Joan Cooke. Joan had gone out on the lake in another boat, and had swum over to get in the *Mipepa*.

Joan had been yelling encouragement to Marilyn, joining Gus and the chorus of George and young Peter. But then Gus asked her to do something that no one else could do — join Marilyn in the water.

"I can't swim in slacks and a blouse," Joan exclaimed.

"Take them off," Gus responded. "Get those outer clothes off, Joan," he said, "and get in there and swim with the kid!"

It was, like every suggestion from Gus Ryder, an order — and Joan, as a true member of the Lakeshore Swimming Club, was duty-bound to obey. For a moment, Joan hesitated. She gazed at the flotilla of boats that had gathered around Marilyn. There were at least 20 boats, some small, some very large. They were loaded with friends, other swimmers, curious on-lookers, and dozens of reporters and photographers sent to cover the story — all those boats, all those people, all those cameras.

George Bryant saw the uncertainty in Joan's eyes. "They won't take a picture of you," he said.

Assured, Joan removed her outer clothes and slipped into the water wearing only her panties and brassiere. She swam over to Marilyn, who was only floating, her strong stroke now reduced to a useless wave of her arms.

Joan was swimming closer and closer to Marilyn, getting almost too close. "Don't touch her, Joan," Gus yelled. "You'll disqualify her!"

The splash of Joan's swimming made Marilyn lift her head and open her eyes. She saw her best friend swimming toward her. She smiled for the first time in hours.

"Come on, you Lakeshore champ," said Joan.

"Give 'em that old Atlantic City fight!"

Suddenly, Marilyn was laughing again.

"C'mon," Joan shouted, "let's go!"

Marilyn and Joan were talking together — and they were swimming together. They were swimming strongly for the shore — stroke, stroke, stroke.

Chapter 6
I Can't Go Any Farther!

The end was near, but Marilyn's race across the lake was far from over. Instead of getting easier, the last part of the swim was going to be the toughest part of all. Marilyn had speeded up her pace when Joan Cooke swam along with her, but Joan didn't stay in the water long. She got back into the *Mipepa* and wrapped herself up in blankets.

Marilyn had worked hard to swim as far as she had. She was within sight of the Toronto shore — but as hard and fast as she swam, the shore was as far away as ever. As Marilyn said later, the city was "like the mechanical rabbit they use for greyhound racing. It never seemed to get any closer."

Part of the reason was just an illusion. From the lake, the city simply appeared closer than it really was — but there was also a great deal of truth in what Marilyn saw. In fact, the city was further away than she thought because the lake's currents were sweeping her off her course. It seemed that for every one hundred metres she swam closer to the shore, the current dragged her two hundred metres further west, away from the CNE. And there was, as usual, one more reason why — once again it was Gus Ryder. His blackboard messages always made it seem the end was just over the next wave.

WE ARE TAKING YOU STRAIGHT IN, he wrote. The message was supposed to encourage Marilyn to resume her fast pace. She had been doing 64 strokes a minute for a while, but now she dropped down to 50 — and there were many moments she dropped right down to zero.

ONE AND A HALF MILES TO GO, Gus wrote — and of course that wasn't true. That would mean they were less than two and a half kilometres from the finish. The reporters in the other boats could read the blackboard and see the shore properly. They guessed they were really more than six kilometres out.

But Gus wouldn't stop with his messages. For a while he let Joan Cooke use the blackboard, and Joan drew funny pictures on it to make Marilyn laugh and keep her happy. She drew cartoon drawings of their friends and some of the other members of the Lakeshore Swimming Club. But Joan and Marilyn soon tired of the cartoons and Gus took over the blackboard once again.

Keeping Marilyn focused on the swim was serious business. It was impossible to talk to her now. The blackboard was the only way to reach her.

Marilyn had stopped once again — the pauses were coming more often and were lasting longer. Sometimes Gus would use the stick and extend another paper cup of corn syrup mixed with Pablum, and other times he'd write yet another message on the blackboard. When she stopped she would turn to the *Mipepa*, and Gus and the others would have a clear view of her tired face. Marilyn seemed unable to comprehend what was going on around her. She stared blankly at Gus.

Gus wrote another message — IF YOU QUIT, I QUIT. Without a change in her dazed expression, Marilyn turned away and began to swim once more.

The whole city — in fact, the entire country — now knew about Marilyn's struggle as she swam slowly to the shore — stroke after stroke after stroke. Newspapers had printed extra editions with big headlines about her swim. Early in the afternoon, the *Star* put out an edition with a big headline, FOUR MILES TO GO. Not long after, the *Tely* responded with one that declared, ONLY YARDS TO GO. Radio stations had reporters in the flotilla of boats that had gathered around the *Mipepa*. The *Toronto Star* had hired two airplanes with floats instead of wheels so they could land on the water — reporters and photographers were flown out to get the story. The *Telegram* had an airplane too, as well as boatloads of reporters following Marilyn and the *Mipepa*.

The competition to cover the story of Marilyn's swim across Lake Ontario was intense, and led to many bizarre — and dangerous — incidents on the water.

The reporters and editors at the *Telegram* were surprised by the public interest in the Marilyn's story — and were rankled that the exclusive story that Gus Ryder had offered them, and that their publisher had rejected, was now supposed to be an exclusive report in the *Star*. It was a tradition at the *Tely* to hate the *Star*, and for reporters to do anything they could to beat the *Star* to the story. In extreme cases, *Tely* reporters would literally kidnap someone to keep them out of reach of *Star* reporters. They weren't mean about it — in fact, they were perfectly charming and overwhelmingly generous.

To get a few precious personal details for a big story — perhaps involving a robbery or a murder — they'd find someone who knew the victim or the suspect, someone who would talk. Then they'd invite the person who had the information to move into a luxury hotel, at the *Tely*'s expense, for a day or two — just long enough to keep them from talking to the *Star*. The *Tely* reporters would interview the person, squeeze out every last drop of "human interest" information, run the exclusive story on page one, and send the person back home in a taxi.

It wouldn't take very long for the *Tely* team to cook up a plan to kidnap Marilyn Bell. They would do anything to steal the so-called "exclusive" story from the *Star*.

The battle for the story began on the water. The *Star* had George Bryant in the *Mipepa* and a crew of other reporters and photographers following in another boat. The first group from the *Tely* came on the *Ja-Su*, which the CNE had outfitted as a press boat for newspaper writers, photographers, radio reporters, and newsreel cameramen.

The *Ja-Su* kept a respectful distance back from the *Mipepa*, so as not to interfere with Marilyn — but that wasn't good enough for the *Tely* photographers. They wanted to be closer, so they got into a small dinghy and rowed over to take some close-up pictures of the young swimmer.

The *Tely* photographers were frustrated to discover that Marilyn was swimming close by the *Mipepa*, and right alongside the *Mipepa* were two boats from the *Star* — it was almost impossible to take a photograph of Marilyn and Gus without including the boats from the hated *Star* in the background.

Later, the *Tely* sent more reporters in another boat. As the *Tely* boat approached the great convoy of watercraft, it tried to get closer to Marilyn by squeezing between two *Star* boats. This was in the heat of the day and tempers were running as high as the temperature. Someone threw a bottle that whizzed by the head of a newsreel cameraman. There was talk of ramming the other boat, but cooler heads prevailed —though, at one point, the *Ja-Su* and a *Star* boat actually bumped one another. No one was injured, but it was a shocking breach of sailing etiquette. The *Star* later declared that the accident occurred while its boat was attempting to protect Marilyn from "eager fools in powerboats" who were endangering her life and stirring up the water.

As the day went on, the flotilla following Marilyn grew much larger and much weirder. When she started on the New York side of the lake, there were just two boats, the tiny *Mipepa* with Jack at the controls, along with Gus, George, and young Peter. And following close all the way was the *Mona IV*, the larger yacht that carried Marilyn's Mom and Dad, as well as many friends.

By mid-afternoon there was a sprawling convoy.

Joining the boats sent out by CNE, the *Star* and the *Tely*, were many private boats. Toronto's most famous harbour tug, the *Ned Hanlan*, was there, puffing great clouds of black smoke. Boaters came in all sorts of craft from as far away as Hamilton. In one small motorboat was a group of adults and two young boys staring over the side at Marilyn. There was another boat filled with men in business suits, with just one woman who had with her a year-old baby dressed all in pink. Tagging along on the edge of the mass of the flotilla were people in sailboats, kayaks, canoes, and rowboats.

On some boats, especially boats with several reporters on board, there was a holiday atmosphere. One of the strangest sights during the mid-lake portion of the swim, recalled Buck Johnston, a *Star* reporter, was the squadron of floatplanes that joined in. Johnston described how strange it seemed to see, "empty float planes drifting on the lake's surface" behind the boats.

"These were aircraft chartered by the three Toronto newspapers, the CBC, and whatever," he said. "While the pilots were waiting, they were ferried to the adjacent yachts where great parties were going on."

The Toronto Harbour Commission saw the slow-moving fleet growing rapidly and soon became concerned. There she was, a young girl, swimming with an uncontrolled mass of boats swirling around her, and there was nobody really able to take care of her if any-thing should go wrong — and since she was swimming in the water administered by the Harbour Commission, it was ultimately responsible for her well-being. The Commission sent not one, but two dinghies — with two lifeguards in each boat — to row alongside Marilyn and make sure she was safe.

The boats could be a danger, but they also kept Gus in touch with what was happening elsewhere in the race. The boats had radios and could receive messages from shore and from other boats. That's how Gus had learned about Florence Chadwick quitting, and then about Winnie Roach Leuszler. As he watched Marilyn bravely battling the waves, he heard someone yell to him from the *Ned Hanlan* — it was the officer who had been tending the tug's radio. He had a megaphone. "She's been offered another $6000," he shouted. That brought the total prize money to $15,000, an astonish-ing amount.

This was a message for Marilyn.

NOW $15,000, Gus wrote on his blackboard. Marilyn was on the edge of complete collapse. Her arms were moving, but she was simply too tired to notice the sign.

Some of the powerful motorboats were churning the water, creating waves in their wake. To keep them away from his daughter, Syd Bell went to the prow of the *Mona IV*, yelling at some of the boat operators and even throwing bottles at some as a warning.

Among the managers of the CNE, emotions were running almost as high. After Marilyn became caught in the powerful currents in Lake Ontario, people began to realize that it would be very difficult for her to swim up to the shore by Exhibition Park. However, the CNE managers still wanted her to try. They wanted to give her a grand reception there.

One of the first to figure out that the CNE's plans were about to be ignored was a photographer with the *Tely*. "I don't think those *Star* guys are going to let her land at the Ex," he exclaimed. "She's swimming straight for Sunnyside!"

Allan Lamport, a member of the CNE Sports Committee, heard the *Tely* photographer's remark and looked to the shore. "We'll get her all right," he said.

In those days, before the area became overrun by major traffic highways, Sunnyside was one of Toronto's favourite parks, a lakeside wonderland of pavilions and pools and summer amusements. From the various boats that were in the flotilla following Marilyn, Gus and the onlookers could now see the gaily lit buildings at Sunnyside quite clearly.

Lamport shouted over to Gus. "Isn't it just as close

to take her to the Ex? We've got a crowd waiting there for you," he yelled.

"We can't get in there," Gus called back. "She's going against the waves." The sun had set and the sky was darkening. The Harbour Commissioner, W. H. Bosley, heard the exchange. "The poor girl," he said. "I hope this isn't going to hurt her."

Lamport wouldn't give up. "Gus," he shouted, "you're headed for the widest part of the bay!"

Gus ignored him. He turned his attention back to the tired schoolgirl in the water.

"Swim for the yellow building, Marilyn," he said, "the yellow building, Marilyn." He said it softly, but Lamport heard what he said — and understood what it meant.

"No, no," shouted Lamport.

"Keep quiet!" Gus ordered. "We're running this."

Lamport wasn't the only CNE official upset by Marilyn's change in course. Another speedboat joined the flotilla with three more CNE officials on board — Robert Saunders, the president, along with Sports Director George Duthie and General Manager Hiram MacCallum. They pulled up alongside the *Star* yacht.

Duthie was first to call out. "Have her swim to the Ex," he shouted. "We've got a pot of earth there she's to touch."

I Can't Go Any Farther!

A *Star* reporter answered back: "She'll land wherever she can!"

The response stunned the CNE officials. "Is this a *Toronto Star* swim?" Saunders demanded.

"The CNE had nothing at all to do with this swim," a *Star* reporter yelled back.

Tensions were mounting in the darkening gloom of the evening. The CNE boat began coming in closer and closer. Once again Syd Bell became the protective champion of his brave daughter. As the CNE boat pulled up, he roared, "You get out of here!"

The CNE officials might think they could challenge the reporters and photographers of the *Toronto Star*, but there was no way they were willing to risk a dispute with Syd Bell. They pulled back and kept their distance.

Then it happened — Marilyn Bell reached her limit. It was 6:36 p.m. Marilyn stopped swimming. It took all her energy just to stay afloat. The lifeguards in the dinghies stopped their oars and kept a sharp eye on her, ready to jump in and rescue the tired girl.

"Come on," Gus said, as he had a thousand times before. "Keep going!"

The response from the girl in the water was heart-rending. "I'm tired," was all she could say. It wasn't a statement, it was a wail, a cry for sympathy, a plea for help.

"Come on," said Joan Cooke, "15 minutes more!"

But Marilyn couldn't swim another single minute more, much less 15.

"I can't go any farther," she said.

Everyone watched Marilyn. "Come on," yelled George Bryant, "only a little more!"

Then Syd Bell stepped forward once more to defend his daughter. The time had finally come to end the pain.

"Take her out, Gus!" Syd shouted.

But Gus didn't hear what Syd yelled — or perhaps he chose not to hear it.

"Fifteen minutes more, Marilyn," is what Gus said. "Come on!"

And once again Marilyn Bell responded to the command she couldn't refuse. She put her face back down in the water and began to stroke toward the shore. She wasn't sure of anything except pain. Everything ached. There were voices she could hear, coming from somewhere, saying over and over again, "The yellow building, the yellow building."

She stopped again. Gus grabbed his stick and loaded up another paper cup, pouring into it the very last drop of corn syrup on board the *Mipepa*. More than anything, Marilyn needed sleep, but that was something she couldn't have, not yet — instead, Gus gave her one final paper cup full of instant energy.

Marilyn and Gus had been through so much together. Gus looked into her face and asked the one question that everyone else wanted him to ask ages ago: "Do you want to come out?"

Marilyn Bell answered Gus Ryder in the only way that a Lakeshore Swimming Club champion could. There was no strength in her voice, but there was a wee bit of power left in her arms.

"Which way do I go?" she asked, and she began swimming once again — stroke, stroke, stroke.

Lamport and other CNE officials were furious. "Gus had got a mad on for the Ex," Lamport snarled, "you can see that!" The Exhibition grounds were just a mile to the east and were packed solid with people, all anxiously awaiting Marilyn.

The night was getting cold. Those who had them, pulled on extra sweaters and jackets. Perhaps the least prepared for a cold night was one of the lifeguards from the Toronto Harbour Commission who had arrived shirtless, wearing only his swimming suit.

It was also getting quite dark, although the moon helped. The grand flotilla of boats that swarmed around Marilyn began to turn on their running lights — from shore it looked like a swarming mass of glowing insects was hovering over the water.

No longer was it easy to see Marilyn. She was swallowed up in the darkness — but from time to time, her white swimming cap could be seen bobbing in the waves. And from time to time, the voice of Gus Ryder could be heard.

At 7:50 p.m. his voice sounded hoarse. No longer did his commands boom over the water.

"Come on, Marilyn," he said, "10 minutes more!"

The Harbour Commissioner grew more concerned at Marilyn's slow progress. He made a ruling that helped end the torture sooner. "If she touches the breakwater," he declared, "that's sufficient." The breakwater was about 140 metres from the actual shore. Marilyn would not have to swim over the submerged breakwater, across the lagoon area, and touch the shore — which was crowded with an unbelievable mass of people, all of them cheering.

Someone on the *Star* boat passed the word on to Gus.

"When your boat touches the sea wall, bring her right here. Don't let her get up, just touch!"

Gus took his flashlight and shone the beam of light forward. He could see Marilyn was just seconds from touching the breakwater. The captain of a nearby motor launch sounded his horn to celebrate the impending victory — suddenly the night was alive with a cacophony of sirens and bells and whistles. The crowd on the shore couldn't see what was happening — they didn't know that Marilyn still hadn't touched the breakwater yet — but they joined in shouting and cheering. Grown men shouted like schoolboys, tears streaming down their cheeks.

Gus could see the breakwater. Marilyn was moving slowly forward toward the goal. He signaled to Jack to pull the *Mipepa* back so Marilyn could approach the breakwater all by herself.

All alone, Marilyn Bell reached out to touch the breakwater. This would be her victory — after all, it was she alone who did all the swimming, all the way across Lake Ontario. Gus Ryder was just her coach.

Chapter 7
Congratulations — For Finishing the Swim!

hat happened after she stretched forward to touch the breakwater was never clear in Marilyn's mind. She had been in the water too long. She was too tired to separate the minutes and seconds, too exhausted to notice what was going on around her. It was all a foggy blur, like a dream. The dream became a nightmare when the lake's strong currents added to her agony. She was now 52 kilometres from her starting point in New York State, but thanks to the treacherous currents, she'd been forced to swim 64 kilometres, possibly much more. In this dream she had been swimming for 20 hours and 59 minutes.

Congratulations — For Finishing the Swim!

The time was 8:06 p.m. The nightmare — and the pain — was about to end.

At the very instant Marilyn Bell touched the breakwater, a great chain of very strange events was unleashed. Marilyn was able to see some of it, but would not know about many other things until much later.

There was so much confusion. It came as a great surprise to Marilyn, for instance, when two of the lifeguards from the Harbour Commission came to her as soon as she touched the breakwater. They were the first ones to reach her. The *Mipepa* and all the other boats had stayed back. The lifeguards began to pull her out of the water. She wasn't grateful for their assistance — she was furious at their interference!

"Let me go!" Marilyn shouted at them. "I'm all right!" she said. The Harbour Commission lifeguards stopped tugging at her, stunned by her outburst.

She pushed the lifeguards away and started swimming again. Jack gave the *Mipepa* a wee twist of the throttle and pulled up beside her. Joan and George leaned out to help Marilyn into the boat.

Marilyn finally realized she didn't have to swim any more and began to notice the pandemonium going on all around her — thousands of people cheering, sirens wailing, bells ringing, horns honking, and bright flares shooting up and setting fire to the sky.

Marilyn Bell

All this was for Marilyn Bell. All this because a young girl had managed to swim across Lake Ontario, when all others had failed. She couldn't believe it. It was overwhelming. She had no idea people cared so much. Marilyn had heard applause after winning races, but it wasn't like this. And it was nothing like this when she came home from Atlantic City after winning the Centennial Marathon; there were only a few friends at the airport to meet her and the other Lakeshore Swimming Club members. The public had never paid any attention to her or the other swimmers, not like this. Nothing could be like this.

Marilyn looked around in amazement at the roaring hordes.

"Are these people crazy?" she asked in a whisper as Gus and George pulled her aboard the *Mipepa.* "Or am I?"

It was a raucous and crazy scene — and it was about to get crazier. There was something about Marilyn's victory that made some people do things they might not otherwise do. Just moments before, as Marilyn had come up to the concrete wall of the breakwater, for instance, some people were so excited that they jumped in the water in their clothes, so they could be there at the very moment she touched the wall. One man even grabbed at her swimsuit and was trying to cut off a piece as a souvenir! George stood up in the *Mipepa*

Congratulations — For Finishing the Swim!

Gus congratulates Marilyn

with an oar and swung it around to keep the crazies away.

Once Gus and George had Marilyn safely in the *Mipepa*, Jack took them over to the *Star* boat, the *Mona IV*, where Marilyn's parents were waiting for her. Her Mom and Dad hugged her dearly and then helped her get to bed in one of the bunks in the boat.

But Marilyn couldn't rest — not right away. Her body had been working too hard for too long. She ached all over. She was sitting up in the bunk, sipping on a cup of hot cocoa, when she realized she couldn't feel her legs. Her mind was playing little tricks. Somehow, Marilyn began to believe that she was paralyzed.

"I can't walk!" she cried out. "I can't feel my legs!"

Her mother tried to calm her, but Marilyn was in no mood to be reassured. She was frantic with fear. Words wouldn't work. Marilyn needed proof.

"Sure you can, honey," her mother said. She put her arm around Marilyn and helped her out of the bunk, then walked around the tiny cabin with her. The simple movement — just getting up and taking a few steps with Mom — did the trick. Marilyn calmed down. The fear melted away and Marilyn got back on the bunk.

Outside, the crowd of thousands milled about in all directions. Only a few really knew where Marilyn was and where she was going. The special grandstand the

CNE had built facing the water at the Exhibition grounds was still packed with thousands of spectators expectantly waiting to see the girl who had crossed the lake. Among the noisiest in the crowd were Marilyn's classmates from the Loretto school.

"One, two, three, four! Who are we for!" they chanted. "Marilyn! Marilyn! Rah! Rah! Rah!"

A sudden sound from the public address system brought an immediate silence to the crowd.

"We regret," declared the anonymous voice, "that Marilyn Bell's condition does not permit her to receive her admirers." Disappointed, the spectators began drifting out into the equally crowded Exhibition grounds. The total crowd that had gathered at the Ex and along the Sunnyside shores was estimated to be more than 250,000, the largest number ever assembled in Toronto. It would be many hours before most of them would get home.

Newsboys were already shouting out the news that Marilyn had won her race. The *Star* had printed a special edition in advance with a screaming headline: MARILYN MAKES IT!

Trucks from both the *Star* and *Tely*, all loaded full with the special editions, had been parked near the Exhibition ready for Marilyn's arrival. Toronto's other big paper, the *Globe and Mail*, was a morning newspaper.

Rather than wait for the next day to run the story, however, the *Globe* reporters filled their pre-midnight first edition, affectionately called the Bulldog edition by reporters, with Marilyn's story. Usually, most copies of the Bulldog were sent to out-of-town news stands and subscribers, but this night thousands of extra copies were printed and trucked to newsboys at the Ex.

While the reporters, photographers, and editors were all proud of their extra editions, however, the crew from the *Tely* knew that the game was really just beginning. The *Star* reporters believed they had the exclusive story of Marilyn's completely wrapped up — after all, the *Star* was the only newspaper that had a reporter at Marilyn's side all the time she was swimming. And now the young girl was travelling in a *Star* boat, the *Mona IV*, over to a dock selected by the *Star*. Then she would be taken in a *Star*-ordered ambulance to the Royal York Hotel, where she would be checked over by a doctor hired by the *Star*, and where a special room reserved by the *Star* awaited the tired swimmer. The *Star* had thought of everything.

All this was true — the *Star* did have a commanding advantage over the *Telegram* and all other newspapers. But as the *Star* was soon to learn, the *Tely* had something that the *Star* was lacking, and that was the ruthless determination to get the story — at any price.

Congratulations — For Finishing the Swim!

While the *Star* editors waited complacently for the reporters to file their stories, the *Tely* editors had been frantically plotting, concocting outrageous tricks and ploys to outdo the *Star* with their story of Marilyn's swim across the lake. And, yes — they really were planning to kidnap her away so the *Star* reporters couldn't get to her.

The *Star* reporters and photographers set out to play it straight. The *Tely* team was ready to bend the rules and, if necessary, to break the rules entirely — anything to get the story.

The *Tely* also had a bit of luck on its side. The *Star* did have a reporter, George Bryant, in the *Mipepa* from the very start, but for some reason, in all the excitement and confusion of the race, George had forgotten to keep a notebook. He had travelled all the way across the lake with Marilyn and Gus, and had heard every dramatic exchange between the brave swimmer and her coach, but he hadn't written down a single word.

George had brought a camera, it was true, and had taken many pictures along the way. But George ran out of film long before the finish. It was an enterprising *Tely* photographer, Ted Dinsmore, who scrambled out on the edge of the breakwater, elbowed his way through a small crowd of onlookers, and snapped the one and only picture that was ever taken of the tired little girl actually touching the breakwater to end her race. Dinsmore's photo of Marilyn took up most of page one in the next day's *Tely*.

The *Tely* reporters had got word of most of the *Star*'s plans, and even knew the room number at the Royal York that the *Star* had reserved for Marilyn. They set out to beat the *Star* in any way they could. A *Tely* reporter had been listening in on the *Star*'s radiophone frequency, and had learned the secret location where the Star planned to meet Marilyn with its ambulance. That's why one group of *Tely* staffers was sent to the dock at the Toronto Lifesavers' Station. In case the *Star* made a sudden change to the plans, and sent Marilyn somewhere else, the *Tely* was ready — another *Tely* team had been sent to wait at the National Yacht Club, and there was a team at each of the four entrances to the Royal York Hotel. Another small squad was sent over to the King Edward Hotel, just in case, and one more group was stationed at the Bell home out in New Toronto.

The boldest part of the *Tely* plot was to literally sneak Marilyn away from the *Star* reporters. The *Tely* knew all about the *Star*'s ambulance, so the *Tely* crew hired one of their own. One of the *Tely*'s top writers, Dorothy Howarth, got herself a nurse's uniform and rode along in the ambulance. The *Tely* also had a large room reserved at the Royal York Hotel — reserved for Marilyn Bell.

Congratulations — For Finishing the Swim!

On the way to the Lifesavers' Station, the *Tely* ambulance got caught in heavy traffic along the waterfront. One of the reporters told the ambulance driver to turn on the flashing emergency lights and start the siren wailing. Instantly, pedestrians and other drivers scrambled to get out of the way — everyone, even police officers sent to control the traffic, assumed that the ambulance had Marilyn Bell inside. The *Tely* reporters kept their heads down low as the police waved the ambulance through crowded intersections. The crowd by the roadside cheered as the ambulance roared away. Off it went — straight to the Lifesavers' Station dock.

It wasn't easy for the *Mona IV* to get to the dock. Hundreds of spectators were on boats in the harbour, blocking the *Mona IV*'s passage. The harbour was as crowded as the shore. Slowly, the *Mona IV* worked its way through the clutter of boats and came up to the dock at the Lifesavers' Station. Buck Johnston, one of the *Star* reporters on board, was shocked to see how many people were waiting for them at the dock — especially how many reporters and photographers there were from the *Tely*. The *Tely* ambulance was there waiting, front and centre, with "nurse" Dorothy Howarth standing by with a couple of stretcher carriers.

The *Tely* ambulance was soon put out of commission, however. Reporters from the *Star* saw the keys hanging in the ignition. They reached in and grabbed the keys and tossed them away — then they opened the hood, and pulled out the ignition wires so the engine wouldn't start, even if someone had a spare key.

Then the *Star* ambulance rolled up. The *Tely*'s plan to kidnap Marilyn had been foiled, but the *Tely* team was not ready to give up yet.

The *Mona IV* wouldn't tie up until *Tely* reporters and photographers were removed from the dock. Once again, it was Syd Bell who had to take control of the situation for his daughter's safety. He asked Ed Hopkins, an official with the Harbour Commission, to clear the dock of all the *Tely* reporters. The only ones allowed to greet Marilyn on the dock would be "friends, relatives, and the *Star*."

Hopkins asked the *Tely* crew to leave but they flatly refused to move. They stayed in place until 12 police constables were called. The police moved them on, but as soon as they could, the *Tely* members crept back, hiding behind posts and barrels. There they waited until they could see Marilyn.

Waiting on the boat, Marilyn herself got into the spirit of the game. She asked a *Star* reporter if she should disguise herself. "Would you like me to put a blanket over my head so they can't get pictures?" she asked. The reporter pondered her suggestion for a moment, then declined the offer. Instead, Marilyn came off the boat with her head held high. She was wearing a two-piece sweat suit. She went straight to the stretcher that the *Star* had waiting for her. As the stretcher-bearers carried Marilyn to the ambulance, the *Tely* reporters and photographers jumped out of hiding and began yelling out questions to Marilyn and Gus. Flashguns exploded as the photographers snapped pictures. They crowded around the stretcher, bumping and jostling — the stretcher went down and a reporter fell on top of Marilyn. He was quickly pulled off and Marilyn was not hurt.

The stretcher-bearers hurried to the ambulance. As they were loading Marilyn into the back, a *Tely* photographer popped up out of a nearby barrel and began flashing pictures. Buck Johnston of the *Star* saw him and kicked the barrel, knocking it over and sending the *Tely* photographer tumbling.

Just as the ambulance doors were being closed, *Tely* "nurse" Dorothy Howarth climbed in beside Marilyn. Not recognizing her, a *Star* reporter had actually helped Dorothy into the ambulance — but he soon realized his mistake. "Get outa there, you!" he commanded. Dorothy got out much faster than she got in.

The *Star* had a plan to avoid any interference from the *Tely* and other newspapers — it was a plan doomed to fail. The ambulance carried Marilyn swiftly to the Royal York Hotel, and pulled around the back to the hotel's freight entrance. Marilyn was taken on the stretcher to a waiting freight elevator. Buck Johnston from the *Star* was at her side. He would accompany her all the way to her room.

There was a man holding the freight elevator ready for Marilyn. Buck Johnston assumed the man was a hotel employee, but he was mistaken. The man started asking Marilyn questions — he wasn't with the hotel, he was a reporter from the *Tely!* Buck Johnston ordered the man to get out.

The elevator went down into the basement of the Royal York. The door opened and Marilyn was surrounded by a hundred hotel staff members — chambermaids, porters, bellboys, cooks, waiters, and waitresses gathered around, cheering and applauding their famous guest.

The stretcher was pushed through the crowd in the basement to another elevator, this one a regular passenger elevator that would take Marilyn upstairs to her room on the fourth floor. Again, when the elevator opened, Marilyn was surrounded — but, this time, not by hotel staff. Waiting for her in the hallway were dozens of reporters and photographers from the *Tely* and other newspapers, plus magazines and radio stations — they all immediately began shouting out more questions and snapping more photographs.

It seemed to take forever, but finally the stretcher and its sleepy passenger made it through the jostling crowd of reporters down the hall to Marilyn's room.

When they got in the room, Buck Johnston and the other *Star* reporters spotted yet one more stranger waiting there for Marilyn — and they were certain he must be yet another *Tely* reporter. They insisted he leave — and right now.

But for once it wasn't a *Tely* reporter. He wasn't a reporter at all. He was Johnny Johnston, the manager of the Royal York Hotel. "I only want to shake the hand of this brave, young lady," he said. Marilyn smiled at him.

Also waiting in the room was Dr. Frank Griffin, the doctor hired by the *Star*. It didn't take him long to check Marilyn and give her a clean bill of health.

"It's absolutely fantastic," he exclaimed. "I've never seen anything like it. After such an ordeal," he said, "you can expect a lowering of blood pressure. But hers is absolutely normal. I would say this is a surprise to the medical profession."

Finally, they all left. Finally, the *Star* reporters and photographers went to the newspaper office. Finally, the doctor closed his bag and went away. Finally, Marilyn was left alone. Finally, she could fall asleep.

She had no idea what was going to happen to her tomorrow — she was too tired to care.

As Marilyn slept, the reporters at the *Tely* were working overtime. Over at the *Star* office, it was business as usual. The editors knew that George Bryant was going to interview Marilyn in the morning and would have a story for the afternoon edition. The *Tely* team had failed with their crazy kidnap caper, but they weren't through playing tricks. They knew the *Star* had exclusive rights to Marilyn's personal story — but no one, not even the *Star* and its exclusive contract, could stop the *Tely* from coming up with a story of its own.

And what a story the *Tely* came up with! No matter where they were assigned — to a boat on the lake, in the crowd on the waterfront, or listening in on radio messages — all the *Tely* reporters were instructed to write down every little scrap of information they could. When they saw Gus scribble a message on his blackboard, they would copy it down. When they heard Gus shout to Marilyn, they wrote down what he said — and then they wrote down what she answered.

And in the midst of that hubbub when Marilyn finally landed on the dock, and when she arrived at the hotel, they did get a few brief answers to the barrage of questions they shouted at Marilyn. Poor George Bryant got into the *Mipepa* without a notebook, and got out of the boat without a single quote to work into his story. But when the *Tely* reporters got back to their newspaper office, their notebooks were overflowing with little facts and fragments, wee snippets of overheard conversations, and a few direct responses to their many questions.

All the information was dumped on the desk of Dorothy Howarth, the reporter who had dressed up in a nurse's white uniform. Dorothy was a very talented writer, one of the best on the *Tely* staff when it came to human-interest stories.

Dorothy set to work. She assembled all the scraps of information and wrote the story as if it had been written by Marilyn herself.

Then, to complete the illusion, another *Tely* reporter was sent out to see Marilyn's teachers at the Lorreto College School. As *Tely* Publisher John Basset delighted in describing the mission in years to come, the editors sent "some good Catholic boy to sweet talk the Sisters." However he did it, the reporter certainly accomplished his mission — he returned from the school with some of Marilyn's personal belongings.

One of the things the reporter got was a schoolbook, and inside the front cover was what the editors were really looking for — Marilyn had written her name in the book. The editors had the signature photocopied so it could be printed in the newspaper.

There it was for all the world to see, especially everyone over at the *Star*. The *Tely* had a huge headline proclaiming: MARILYN'S STORY — I FELT I WAS SWIMMING FOREVER. And right beneath it was Marilyn's signature and the story that Dorothy had concocted.

Dorothy did an exceptional job and turned in a much better story than George Bryant was able to write for the *Star*. Few in the general public cared how it was done, but in the newspaper business, the *Tely*'s story sparked endless debates about journalistic ethics. As for what Marilyn Bell thought about it, she said later, "I liked my story better in the *Tely* than in the *Star*."

Her story wasn't over, however — in a way, it was just beginning. On the morning after her swim, Marilyn woke up to discover that she was a celebrity in Canada — her name was known from coast to coast. It certainly wasn't what she expected. "I thought my swim, if I finished it, would be on the back pages of the papers," she said that morning. "I thought I would just climb out and go home and a few of my friends would congratulate me."

In the days to come, Marilyn received a deluge of gifts from well-wishers. The gifts were worth thousands of dollars and included a new convertible car, a TV set, a record player, several radios, typewriters, luggage, a basket of apples, lots of clothes, furniture, and a truckload of kitchen appliances, cutlery, and dinnerware. There was even a chirping budgie in a cage. She was invited to be on radio shows and appear on television. There were portraits of her in magazines. The city of Toronto had a grand tickertape parade for her through the downtown streets — she and Gus rode together in an open car, waving to cheering people crowded on both sides of the street. Just because she swam across the lake, everyone wanted to cheer and congratulate her.

Somehow, though, of all the times that she received congratulations, there was one occasion that always stood out — and meant more than all the rest. It happened that very night, shortly after Marilyn was lifted out of the water.

It happened while Marilyn was still groggy, still tired, and absolutely bewildered by all the craziness going on around her — reporters shouting questions at her, photographers jumping out of nowhere to take her picture. Marilyn had just got off the *Mona IV* and was resting on the stretcher in the ambulance. In a moment the ambulance was going to take her away to the Royal York Hotel.

Suddenly there was someone next to her in the ambulance that Marilyn was very happy to see. It was her best friend, Joan Cooke. Joan gave Marilyn a big hug.

"That was wonderful, Marilyn!" Joan said.

"Congratulations!"

Marilyn was mystified. What was Joan talking about?

She looked at Joan and asked, "For what?"

Now it was Joan's turn to be mystified.

"For the swim," Joan said, "for finishing the swim."

Now the mystery was solved. Now Marilyn finally understood why so many people were so excited.

"I did?" Marilyn said. "I finished?"

Until that moment she hadn't known. No one had ever mentioned to her that the breakwater was the finish line.

Once again Marilyn was the last one to know. She was the last to know about Florence Chadwick, and the last to know about Winnie Roach Leuszler.

Now Marilyn Bell was the last to know about herself. But finally, more than ever before, now she knew she was a true Lakeshore champion. She was the only one to swim across Lake Ontario.

Epilogue

No one has ever duplicated the drama of Marilyn Bell's swim across Lake Ontario. Some have tried to swim shorter distances to Toronto, from St. Catharines or other starting points, but no one has ever matched the excitement of her success. Perhaps no one ever will, or will even want to — at least, not until the water in Lake Ontario is made as clean as it was in 1954.

The Lakeshore Swimming Club continues but is now called Lakeshore Swim Club — and all its classes are now held in the pool. Gus Ryder finally retired as a coach but continued to be a strong supporter of safe swimming until his death in 1991.

For a time, Marilyn Bell continued her long-distance swims. She became the youngest person to cross the English Channel and also swam across the Strait of Juan de Fuca between Vancouver Island and Washington State.

Then, other interests entered her life. The most important was the handsome lifeguard, Joe DiLascio, she had met at the Atlantic City Centennial Marathon. They married and raised four children in New Jersey. In

2002 she was made a Member of the Order of Ontario, the highest honour the province can bestow.

Bibliography

Callwood, Joan. "How Marilyn Bell Swam Lake Ontario." (*Maclean's Magazine*; November 1, 1954.) reprinted in *Canada in the Fifties: From the Archives of Maclean's*. Viking. 1999.

Doyle, Richard. *Hurly-Burly, A Time at The Globe*. Macmillan of Canada. 1990.

McAllister, Ron. *Swim to Glory: The Story of Marilyn Bell and the Lakeshore Swimming Club*. McClelland & Stewart. 1954.

Morrow, Don; Keyes, Mary; Cosentino, Frank; Leppage, Ron; Simpson, Wayne. *Concise History of Sport in Canada*. Oxford University Press. 1989.

Sears, Val. *Hello Sweetheart, Get Me Rewrite: Remembering the Great Newspaper Wars*. Key Porter Books. 1988.

Acknowledgments

The author gratefully acknowledges the following sources for quotes contained in this book: the "history-in-a-hurry" quotes published in *The Telegram* and the *Toronto Daily Star*, especially in the editions of September 10, 1954; also June Callwood for "How Marilyn Bell Swam Lake Ontario" in the November 1, 1954 issue of *Maclean's Magazine* and subsequently reprinted in *Canada in the Fifties*; Don Morrow and others who assembled *The Concise History of Sport in Canada*; the redoubtable Val Sears for his raffish account of the *Tely*'s plots and ploys in his memoir, *Hello Sweetheart, Get Me Rewrite*; and Ron McAllister, who put heart and soul into his quickly written classic, *Swim to Glory*. My thanks also go to the many friends in Toronto who described the excitement they felt hearing radio accounts of Marilyn's swim. And, of course, this book simply would not have appeared without the support and patience of Stephen Hutchings and Kara Turner at Altitude; and Michael Rosset at HOMES Publishing Group.

About the Author

Patrick Tivy is the author of two other books by Altitude Publishing. He is also Executive Editor at HOMES Publishing Group of Unionville and is the editor of *Active Adult Magazine, HOMES Magazine* and *Condo Life Magazine*. His home in Toronto is close enough to Lake Ontario that he can hear the waves crash on the shore on stormy nights.

Photo Credits

Cover: Sun Media Corp: **Sun Media Corp:** page 73; *Toronto Star* **file photo:** page 113.

AMAZING STORIES™

GREAT DOG STORIES

Inspirational Tales About
Exceptional Dogs

ANIMAL/HUMAN INTEREST
by Roxanne Willems Snopek

Great Dog Stories
ISBN 1-55153-946-2

AMAZING STORIES
NOW AVAILABLE!

AMAZING STORIES™

TRAILBLAZING SPORTS HEROES

Exceptional Personalities and Outstanding
Achievements in Canadian Sport

HISTORY/SPORT
by Joan Dixon

Trailblazing Sports Heroes
ISBN 1-55153-976-4

Dinosaur Hunters
ISBN 1-55153-982-9

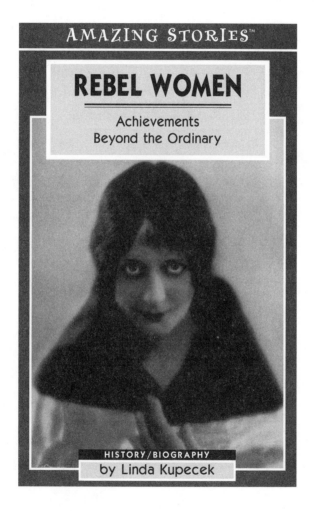

AMAZING STORIES™

REBEL WOMEN

Achievements
Beyond the Ordinary

HISTORY/BIOGRAPHY
by Linda Kupecek

Rebel Women
ISBN 1-55153-991-8

AMAZING STORIES™

THE HALIFAX EXPLOSION

Surviving the Blast that Shook a Nation

HISTORY
by Joyce Glasner

The Halifax Explosion
ISBN 1-55153-942-X

AMAZING STORIES™

EDWIN ALONZO BOYD

The Life and Crimes of Canada's
Master Bank Robber

HISTORY/BIOGRAPHY
by Nate Hendley

Edwin Alonzo Boyd
ISBN 1-55153-968-3

AMAZING STORIES™

SNOWMOBILE ADVENTURES

The Incredible Canadian Success Story
from Bombardier to the Villeneuves

HISTORY/ADVENTURE
by Linda Aksomitis

Snowmobile Adventures
ISBN 1-55153-954-3